T0368792

RICK STEIN'S SIMPLE SUPPERS

RICK STEIN'S SIMPLE SUPPERS

In late June 2022, I had open heart surgery. The morning after the operation, the nurses were urging me to get up and shuffle about the intensive care ward and to cough; this was the worse bit, like the pain of childbirth, perhaps. The other bad thing was having to negotiate with the half a dozen or so tubes going in or coming out of me, so as not to get in a tangle when I tried to stand up.

Even then, in intensive care, a nice Romanian girl came to ask what I wanted to eat for Sunday lunch the next day. The night before the operation they had brought me some haddock fillet that was seasoned with salt and cracked black pepper, then lightly fried, served with a dressing of olive oil, thinly sliced spring onions, diced roasted red peppers, lemon juice and I swear, a touch of soy sauce. It was divine and so simple. Who said hospital food was so terrible? I thought.

So, in my slightly befuddled state from the morphine, I decided to order roast lamb with mint sauce for my Sunday lunch. I'm not that fond of mint sauce, as I find the vinegar spoils the flavour of the lamb. Mint jelly I do like, and I reasoned that nothing could go that wrong with mint sauce. I was wrong. It may have been because my mouth was already very dry, but the lamb was so overcooked that it seemed to stick to the roof of my mouth, and the mint sauce was of a rare consistency, completely gummy with flour.

At the time, I thought this is going to be one of those taste or smell memories that will always take me back with dread to my hospital bed. But at the same time, in my dizzy state, I was thinking positively about getting better and not feeling breathless again, and writing some really simple recipes. I remember I was listening to Steve Winwood's 'Back in the High Life' which includes the following lines:

'I'll be back in the high life again
All the doors I closed one time
Will open up again.'

Having a major operation and surviving it induces mixed feelings of pain and euphoria. I didn't close those doors intentionally, but I sure was looking forward to opening them up again. I decided there and then, light-headedly, to write a cookbook about simple food and how to concentrate on doing simple dishes, like that haddock. The memory of that dish before the operation was as emotional to me as the idea of all those closed doors opening up again. I thought I might just call the book 'Simple Suppers' to suggest not only very straightforward cooking but also informality.

I started remembering the suppers I ate as a child. Things like my dad's clear chicken soup which he'd make on a Sunday night with stock from the lunchtime roast chicken. He'd sprinkle a bit of Parmesan on top – not freshly grated, but from one of those little green cardboard tubs which were all you could get back then. I thought I'd collect a selection of impromptu suppers like a simple summery chicken soup, but I'd also include some rather smart but still simple dishes, like the saltimbocca my mother used to make at my parents' flat in Vicarage Gate in Kensington, London. These were veal escalopes topped with a sage leaf, then wrapped in Parma ham and pinned together with a cocktail stick. They were fried in butter, and she would add a bit of wine to the pan to finish the sauce. It was one of her specialities in the sixties when entertaining friends, such as the Grays from San Francisco, the Ifoulds from Sydney or Karl Finsterbusch from Scarsdale, New York.

A few years earlier, the latter had brought over the complete US top ten for my brother John and me.

There were ten 45s, including 'Not Fade Away' by the Crickets which, aside from Elvis, was the reason that America seemed like the most wonderful place in the world to me.

Thinking about that flat reminded me that once, when my parents were away in Italy, I invited half a dozen school chums to stay one weekend in the Easter holidays so we could go to the Sunset Strip club in Soho. I recall us partly trashing the flat and drinking my dad's samples of rum, gin and whisky from the Distillers Company – he was the MD. When we got to the club, we had to buy champagne, which definitely didn't taste like Coca Cola – more like cherry cola or probably Vimto. The girls were definitely girls, though I don't remember that they took everything off.

Ah, memories – back to my time in hospital. My wife Sas arrived with the biggest bunch of white roses I'd ever seen and commandeered a large vase to put them in in front of the window. She also brought my favourite crumbly fudge which I couldn't eat because it suddenly seemed so aggressively, burningly sweet. I realised later that the Sunday roast lamb had probably been not as terrible as I had thought, but my dreams of lovely simple dishes were made almost more heavenly by the dark memories of that desperately dry lamb and the fudge that burned my throat. As I gazed at the white roses in the window I thought of making something with tomatoes and burrata, a tender gnocchi dish with prawns and basil, and a rocket and fig salad with warm halloumi.

I'm better now but the memory of those days is still there, and I've written this book spurred on by those ideas of keeping it simple. The idea of supper appealed to me because it suggests an ordinary meal, not trying too hard; maybe something you're going to turn out while drinking a glass of vinho verde and listening to 'Once in a Lifetime' by Talking Heads or 'Somewhere Down the Crazy River' by Robbie Robertson. I've included the sorts of things I cook just for myself or for me and Sas, after a walk along the Camel Trail in Cornwall – something like chipotle-glazed pork steaks with sweet potato mash.

Then there are favourites for suppers with family and friends in London, such as a gratin of chicken, leek, cider and potatoes, and some simple fast fish suppers like that haddock. There are a few puds too – easy things like fresh pineapple with chilli or baked pears with ginger nut and almond crunch and my chum Mark Hix's iced berries straight out of the freezer with hot white chocolate sauce.

Perhaps the most overused word in culinary circles is simple. I think it engenders a sort of attitude that persuades people to drop their guard and think that everything is going to be easy. In the same way, the mention of truffle oil in a recipe makes people think everything is going to taste expensive and unforgettable. Every chef has used the word 'simple' in one way or another to describe recipes and here I am using it too. My take on simple suppers is like the analogy of the iceberg or the swimming swan – while some of the recipes are just plain simple, others seem very straightforward but there's a lot more going on underneath.

My aims have been that ideally no dish should take more than an hour of anyone's time to make (many take much less and in the Fast suppers chapter, they're all under half an hour), to keep the number of ingredients down as far as possible, and to never let a recipe go to more than a page. I wanted the ingredients generally, with very few exceptions, to be available from any supermarket, and for the recipes to rely as much as possible on what you might already have in your fridge, freezer and store cupboard. But to do this you need to be organised: first, by having the right ingredients in your pantry and fridge (see pages 262–64 for advice on that, and second, to include some basic ideas that will change a simple dish into something extraordinary, like the bananas with toffee sauce and ice cream on page 260.

I realised I've been guilty in the past of putting time-consuming prep in the ingredient lists to keep the recipe method short, so I decided never to ask for such things as carrots to be cut into 70 x 5mm matchsticks. Just chopping is fine. For the most part I don't specify weights for things like garlic, onions and herbs, unless absolutely necessary, but I have included some guidelines on page 318.

Something I've really enjoyed while writing this book has been looking at ways to save time when cooking the recipes – for example, by making really quick sauces. Everyone likes fish pie but making the béchamel and the mash for the classic version can be time-consuming. I've worked on a simpler method of using cornflour and egg yolks for the sauce and changed the mashed potato to puff pastry. In the croque monsieur I've replaced the béchamel with crème fraiche.

Wherever possible I've cut out stages in making a dish. For instance, any improvement in flavour that you get by sweating onions first, then the garlic, then perhaps chillies, is tiny, so why not save yourself time and cook them all together? I've abandoned peeling and deseeding tomatoes and just chop them. I very rarely finely chop herbs; a rough chop is enough. I've decided to use shop-bought pastry cases rather than make them, as blind baking is a pain in the backside, and my love of bought puff pastry is unabated. I've used it to make a pizza tart rather than using a traditional yeasted dough.

Much against my earlier inclination I've come around to using tins of beans, such as butter beans, haricot, chickpeas and so on, rather than buying them dried, then soaking and cooking them, and I've found that

I really can't tell the difference. I often use frozen fruit instead of fresh, frozen spinach, shop-bought custard, shop-bought stock, bottled mayonnaise and ready-made garam masala. Wherever possible I try to make sure someone else is doing much of the work. I have, though, included my recipes for such things as stocks and mayonnaise at the back of the book should you want them.

I have to say it's been quite a challenge to change my attitude to using prepared ingredients in my cooking when I have spent my lifetime making everything from scratch. The reality is, though, that over the last twenty years what you can buy ready-made has utterly changed in terms of quality and range. What has also changed in that time is the extraordinary belief that we are all terribly busy, so busy that most of the dishes we cook have to be quick and simple.

When I look at my own busy-ness and that of those around me I wonder: what are we doing now that we weren't before? The internet has got a lot to answer for I think, as it's so easy to get involved. My personal time-wasting habit is reading the newspapers online. I look at the *Times*, *Telegraph* and *Guardian* every day and regularly dip into the *Sydney Morning Herald*, plus if I feel like being really irritated, the *Mail Online*. My wife Sas seems to be constantly looking through Instagram, which takes hours but then everyone seems to know what I was doing last Friday. Others spend ages on Wordle, Quordle, Octordle or Nerdle.

All of it seems somehow to be just a distraction, a procrastination – why do we not want to make puff pastry any more? Deep down we know that we'd be happier if we did, but we don't. So simple it is.

FAST SUPPERS

All the dishes in this chapter are not only simple but also designed to be prepared and cooked in under 30 minutes (some in quite a bit less than that. I know you're going to say, 'Whose minutes?' and 'In whose kitchen?', but there's really nothing in them that takes a long time and I make life easy by using things like tins of beans and shop-bought puff pastry.

The temptation when you're tired and hungry, and maybe you've been writing cookery books all day, is to ring for a takeaway or get in your car to go and pick something up. But what I'm saying is that these recipes are quicker – and better – than settling for either of those solutions. If you are anything like me, you might often find takeaways disappointing. They're never quite hot enough and I do get concerned about the presentation of my food. With a takeaway everything has to be squidged into everything else and I worry about the recycling of all that plastic. All in all, you're better off with these recipes.

However, if you are going to cook like this, you do need a slightly extended store cupboard: a supply of things like tinned tomatoes, walnuts, olives and coconut milk and I've written a bit about this in my piece about my pantry (pages 262–264). Stocking up on useful ingredients like these is what makes this kind of cooking quick. Yes, you might have to spend a few pounds, but just think of the hassle of having to rush out to the supermarket to buy the one ingredient you haven't got in your cupboard. And if you have a supply of the basics, such as tins of beans, frozen puff pastry, maybe a jar of harissa, you can always make a meal.

You do need to keep an eye on what you have, though. My problem, and I don't mean to sound like I'm showing off here, is that I've got five store cupboards, because I now have five kitchens, with my latest addition called the summer house, built as a studio kitchen in Padstow.

It's a first-world problem, I know, but I find myself ticking off, say, walnuts in Padstow when I've just bought some in Sydney. Continuing with this theme, another problem is that I wake up in the middle of the night to go for a pee and find myself walking into a wardrobe, because my head is still in the last bedroom.

Returning to store cupboards, I confess that I have an unwillingness to throw away out-of-date jars or tins because I can't bear waste. An example of this came up the last time I made the shakshuka recipe on page 16. I wanted to add some Turkish spicy red pepper paste and glanced at the use-by date on the jar. It was 3/8/2015, so dated from when I made my television series: 'Venice to Istanbul'. Looking at the label on the jar it came as a shock to realise that it came from Gaziantep which was recently hit by a terrible earthquake and it reminded me what a wonderful part of the country that was. I remember when I was there filming, standing on the banks of the Euphrates River and looking into Syria, thinking how much I'd like to film in Aleppo. At that time for a foodie, it would have been a magical place to visit.

Eggs baked in spicy tomato sauce
Shakshuka

SERVES 4
2 tbsp olive oil
1 onion, chopped
2 garlic cloves, chopped
1 red pepper, deseeded and chopped
1 tsp sweet paprika
1 tsp ground cumin
2 x 400g tins of chopped tomatoes
1 tsp chilli flakes
4 eggs
Handful of fresh coriander, chopped
Salt and black pepper

To serve
Crusty bread

In my fridge I have a plastic box of cooked and reduced tomatoes, red peppers, garlic, chilli, onions – whatever is left when I'm about to set out on one of my travels. Written on it in felt-tip pen is 'shakshuka' and it's basically a way of cooking any of those ingredients so they won't spoil while I'm away. Then, when I'm back, all I do is squirt a bit of olive oil into a gratin dish, add a couple of generous serving spoonfuls of the sauce and break in an egg. In winter, just before going for an early morning swim, I turn the oven on. I only swim for a max of ten minutes, so when I get back, into the oven the dish goes. By the time I've had a shower to get some heat back into my system, dressed and put on a jersey, the shakshuka is ready to eat and the hot oven adds a bit of extra warmth to my still slightly chilled body. With a hot cup of coffee, this is the best way to stave off hypothermia. The recipe below is for when I'm making shakshuka from scratch.

Preheat the oven to 190°C/Fan 170°C. Heat the oil in a frying pan and gently soften the onion, garlic and red pepper.

Add the paprika and cumin and fry for a minute, then add the chopped tomatoes and chilli flakes. Cook over a high heat for 4–5 minutes to thicken. Season with salt and pepper.

Pour the mixture into an ovenproof pan. Make 4 hollows with the back of a spoon and break the eggs into them, then bake in the oven for 10 minutes. Alternatively, cover the pan with a lid and cook over a low-medium heat for 7–10 minutes until the eggs are cooked.

Serve sprinkled with coriander and with some bread on the side if you like, to mop up the tomato sauce.

Tomato, mozzarella, black olive & artichoke faux pizza

SERVES 4
2 x 320g ready-rolled puff pastry sheets

Topping
300g tomato sauce, such as Mutti or see p.295
2 x 125–150g mozzarella balls, sliced
Handful of black olives, pitted and halved
8–10 artichoke hearts from a jar, halved
60g Parmesan cheese, freshly grated
Handful of fresh basil leaves
Salt and black pepper

Unless you're experienced at baking pizzas with proper dough there's a lot that can go wrong, as with any yeast-based dish. Most of the time you'd be better off using a roll of ready-made puff pastry as a base. This topping is a particular favourite of mine, using jars of Italian artichoke hearts, tomato sauce and black olives. Here I like to use my favourite Mutti tomato sauce, which is available everywhere, but there's a recipe for home-made tomato sauce on page 295 if you'd prefer to make your own.

Preheat the oven to 230°C/Fan 210°C. Unroll the puff pastry sheets on a couple of baking trays and prick them all over with a fork.

Spread the tomato sauce over the pastry. Top with the mozzarella, olives and artichoke hearts, dividing them equally between the pastry sheets. Add half the grated Parmesan and season with salt and pepper.

Bake for 15–18 minutes, then strew with basil leaves and the rest of the Parmesan and serve immediately.

Baked portobello mushrooms with Dolcelatte & walnuts

SERVES 4
8 large portobello mushrooms
2 garlic cloves, finely chopped
3–4 tbsp olive oil
200g Dolcelatte cheese, chopped or crumbled
4 handfuls of rocket leaves
Handful of parsley, roughly chopped
60g walnuts, roughly chopped
Salt and black pepper

There's almost nothing to do to prepare this dish – just put everything on a baking tray and into the oven. For me, you could put Dolcelatte with almost anything and I'd love it!

Preheat the oven to 200°C/Fan 180°C. Put the mushrooms on a baking tray, underside up. Scatter over the garlic and drizzle with oil, then season with salt and pepper. Divide the Dolcelatte between the mushrooms. Bake for 12–15 minutes, until the mushrooms are tender and the cheese has melted.

Remove the mushrooms and baste them with any juices in the tray. Serve on a bed of rocket, scattered with the parsley and walnuts and with some crusty bread on the side.

Cauliflower, chickpea & coconut curry

SERVES 4
3 tbsp vegetable oil
1 onion, sliced
3 garlic cloves, chopped
15g root ginger, peeled and grated
2 tbsp garam masala
1 tsp ground cumin
1 tsp ground turmeric
¼–½ tsp hot chilli powder
2 x 400g tins of coconut milk
1 heaped tsp sugar
400g tin of chickpeas, drained
1 cauliflower (about 650g), cut into small florets, tender leaves roughly chopped
2 tbsp ground almonds
200g spinach, washed and well drained
Squeeze of lemon juice (optional)
Salt

To serve
Naan
Fresh coriander

This is a dish that Portia Spooner, who works with me on recipes, came up with – living in Totnes, in Devon, she has a lot of vegetarian friends. You may have noticed that Totnes is twinned with Narnia! It's a sort of korma, using coconut milk instead of yoghurt, but like that wonderfully comforting dish from northern India this is very lightly spiced and ever so slightly sweet.

Heat the oil in a large pan and fry the onion, garlic and ginger until light golden brown and softened.

Add the spices and fry for a minute, then add the coconut milk, sugar and chickpeas. Season with salt and simmer for 2–3 minutes. Add the cauliflower and continue to simmer for a further 7–10 minutes until just tender. Stir in the ground almonds and spinach and cook for about 2 minutes until the spinach has wilted.

Add a squeeze of lemon juice, if using, and serve with naan and fresh coriander.

Greek butter beans with spinach, mint & dill

SERVES 4
100ml extra virgin olive oil, plus extra to drizzle
1 onion, finely sliced
1 garlic clove, chopped
300g spinach, washed and well drained or 175g frozen spinach
Small handful of fresh mint
1 tsp dried Greek oregano
Small handful (about 10g) of fresh dill
2 x 400g tins of butter beans, drained and rinsed
200g feta cheese, cubed
Salt and black pepper

To serve
Crusty bread

This is one of those Greek dishes, actually from Corfu, where you find yourself thinking that it's so simple but so good that there must be a secret ingredient that isn't mentioned in the recipe. I find that this is the case with so many Greek dishes; it's all about great produce.

Heat the olive oil in a large wide pan. Add the onion and garlic and cook over a low heat until softened.

Add the spinach and allow it to wilt for 3–4 minutes – you want as much of the liquid from the spinach to evaporate as possible. If you do use frozen spinach, you will need to cook it for a few minutes longer.

Add the herbs and beans, then cook for a further 5–7 minutes until the greens have collapsed and the beans have heated through. Season well with salt and pepper.

Serve with the feta on top and drizzle with a little more oil if desired. Good with crusty bread.

Spaghetti with olive oil & garlic
Spaghetti aglio e olio

SERVES 4

400g spaghetti
80ml olive oil
4 garlic cloves, finely sliced
Large handful of flatleaf parsley, chopped
Chilli flakes (optional)
40g Parmesan, freshly grated, plus extra to serve
Salt and black pepper

When the Spaghetti House chain of restaurants opened in London in the seventies this dish came as something of a revelation to me. Before then, spaghetti always came with lots of sauce, normally involving tomatoes. The idea of just parsley, garlic and olive oil flavouring a bowl of pasta cooked al dente was mind-bendingly trendy, and I still love the dish to this day.

Boil the spaghetti in salted water until al dente, then drain, reserving about a ladleful of the cooking water.

While the pasta is boiling, heat the olive oil in a separate large pan. Add the garlic to the pan and cook for a minute or so, but don't let it brown. Then add the drained spaghetti with the parsley, chilli flakes, if using, and grated Parmesan. Stir to coat the spaghetti, adding some of the reserved pasta water to loosen it if required.

Season with plenty of black pepper and serve with more Parmesan at the table.

Time-saving gadgets

I love a gadget, particularly if it's related to the kitchen in some way, so the recent rise in food prices and inflation generally, which has caused many people to think about more economical ways of cooking, has been a mixture of gloom and excited inventiveness for me.

Having lived through so many gloomy times, I'm reminded of the line from 'Time', a track on Pink Floyd's 'Dark Side of the Moon' album: 'Hanging on in quiet desperation is the English way.' But the upside of that is wasting plenty of time looking online for energy- and time-saving devices. Needless to say, I've now got them all – a pressure cooker, an air fryer, a slow cooker and I've always had a microwave.

I use my microwave all the time for reheating coffee and tea, but it really is good for cooking fish. For defrosting, it's an absolute must and there is no better way of warming tortillas than to pop them in the microwave. But I find the best and most energy efficient use is to par-cook potatoes, sausages or even chicken to then finish off in the oven, in a pan or indeed on a barbecue.

Next, the pressure cooker. I have a pressure cooker in each of my kitchens and at the last count that was five. I know – I keep picking up kitchens like some people pick up classic cars, then I have to buy big sheds to keep them in. The pressure cooker, though, is a fabulous addition that can be kept in your cupboard and used as a normal saucepan when not under pressure. When cooking stocks, pulses, potatoes, stews, curries it saves lots of time – and lots of money. In the old days, there was always the slight worry that a pressure cooker might turn into a bomb sitting on your cooker, but the safety valve always seems to work.

Slow cookers are good for all kinds of soups, curries, stews or stocks, and of course the great advantage is you can get it all going hours before you want to eat it. Make sure you buy one with a timer, though. I may be in a minority, but I hate overcooked meat with a lot of connective tissue. It needs to be cooked to soften the collagen but not for so long that it disintegrates into an oily textureless mush. Another thing to look out for is that some slow cookers have a ceramic insert. Avoid these because you can't brown meat or onions

'The truth is that I really like working with my hands and find it more satisfying than getting out a machine.'

before adding the other ingredients and liquid. Some people say browning isn't necessary, but I think the caramelisation of meat or vegetables adds important flavour and nice colour too. Incidentally, if you have an induction hob you don't really need a slow cooker, as the hob can be turned down very low and each zone has a timer.

The latest and most exciting of these gadgets is the air fryer. Basically, this is a fan-assisted heating element that heats up a small drawer very quickly with the result that you can bake potatoes in forty minutes, roast a whole chicken, albeit a rather small one in forty-five minutes and achieve a fried effect with chips by simply brushing them with oil. It's a misnomer, really, to call it an air fryer because frying essentially means cooking food immersed or semi-immersed in oil, whereas cooking in an air fryer uses very hot air. The great advantages of an air fryer are that much less energy is used than by cooking in an oven, and, as you only brush the food with oil, the finished dishes are far less calorific. The results are fabulous, with really crisp skins on everything.

However, if you want to feed a family of four with plenty of chips, you're going to need a big one. Then you have to ask yourself whether you really want such a large piece of equipment in your small kitchen, or will it find itself in the garage before too long? Mine is already in the garage and although I occasionally bring it into the kitchen, mostly I still use the oven or a pan with some oil in it. In the same way, I often say to myself, shall I get the stand mixer out with the slicing blade or just use a sharp knife and avoid all that extra washing up?

The truth is that I really like working with my hands and I find it more satisfying than getting out a machine. Recently, a man called Nick Edwards, from New South Wales, sent me a knife he'd made. It arrived wrapped up in a hand-stitched hemp sack, the handle is made of Queensland hardwood and the blade of W2 high carbon steel. The balance is perfect, the blade as sharp as ... If you ask me to choose between shredding some cabbage with Nick's knife or in a machine – there's no contest.

Smoked salmon with horseradish cream

SERVES 4

Butter, at room temperature
6 thin slices of wholemeal or rye bread
300–350g smoked salmon
Pinch of cayenne pepper
Chives, snipped
Nonpareille capers
Romaine lettuce

Horseradish cream
175ml crème fraiche
2 tsp creamed horseradish, from a jar
1 tsp Dijon mustard
1 tsp caster sugar
2 tbsp white wine vinegar
Salt

You might say that smoked salmon doesn't really need any accompaniments, apart from a slice of lemon and in my case, a pinch of cayenne pepper. But I have made rather a nice little romaine lettuce salad with horseradish cream that I think goes very well with it. Horseradish with oily fish always works.

Mix together the ingredients for the horseradish cream.

Butter the slices of bread and cut them in half. Arrange the smoked salmon on the bread and sprinkle with cayenne. Scatter over some chives and capers and serve with the horseradish cream and lettuce.

Smoked mackerel paté

SERVES 4–6

225g peppered smoked mackerel fillets, skin and any bones removed
150g cream cheese
25g soft butter
Lemon juice, to taste
1–2 tsp creamed horseradish

To serve
Toast
Green salad

One of our chefs developed this during lockdown to send out as a simple starter in our 'Stein's at Home' food boxes. When you look at how few ingredients there are in this it's amazing how good it tastes. I think it's the combination of the peppered mackerel fillets and the horseradish that make it particularly delicious.

Put the mackerel, cream cheese and soft butter in a food processor and blend to make a paste. Season to taste with lemon juice and horseradish.

Serve with hot toast and a green salad.

Steak burritos

SERVES 4
4 large flour tortillas
300g sirloin or rump steak, at room temperature
Vegetable oil
400g tin of black or kidney beans, drained and rinsed
¼ small red or white cabbage, finely shredded
2 tomatoes sliced
1 ripe avocado, stoned and sliced
100g Cheddar cheese, grated
Small handful of fresh coriander, roughly chopped
Salt and black pepper

To serve
Soured cream, salsa, chilli sauce or mayonnaise

This is another of those dishes where the promise of steak is what makes it sound attractive but the reality is that there is a relatively small amount of meat. It's the other very flavourful ingredients, including black beans, red cabbage, chilli and cheese, that really make it work.

Wrap the tortillas in foil and warm them in the oven at a temperature of about 150°C/Fan 130°C for 5–10 minutes. Alternatively, just put them in the microwave for 30 seconds to soften.

Season the steak with salt and pepper. Brush a frying pan with a little oil and heat over a high heat. Fry the steak for a minute or so on each side, depending on its thickness and how you like your steak, then set it aside on a plate to rest.

Wipe the pan clean and add a tablespoon of oil. Add the kidney beans, season with salt and pepper and warm them through. Slice the steak thinly.

To assemble, lay out 4 pieces of foil or greaseproof paper and top each one with a warmed tortilla. Spoon on some of the beans, add cabbage, slices of steak, tomato and avocado, then sprinkle with cheese and coriander.
Top with your choice of sauce.

Fold up the bottom of each tortilla, then roll up and wrap them in the foil or greaseproof to hold them together.

Chicken satay with peanut sambal & noodles

SERVES 4
600g chicken thigh or breast meat, cut into bite-sized pieces
2 garlic cloves, crushed or grated
Vegetable oil
3 tbsp soy sauce, plus extra to dress the noodles
400g fresh egg noodles
½ cucumber
3 spring onions, finely shredded (see tip)

Sambal
100g crunchy peanut butter
1 garlic clove, crushed or grated
1 tbsp sriracha sauce
Juice of ½ lime
1 tbsp soy sauce
1 tbsp brown sugar
4–5 tbsp just-boiled water

TIP
To make the spring onions into attractive curls as in the photo opposite, cut them into sections of about 6cm long. With a sharp knife, shred them lengthways, drop them into iced water for 5 minutes, then drain.

Many of my flights to Australia have been with Malaysian Airlines. One of the high spots of the trip are the satay sticks they give you before dinner. You get two chicken satays, two beef, a slice of red onion and some thick wedges of cucumber. They are very generous with the sauce, but the slight downside is that you have to use the satay sticks as chopsticks if you want to finish off the sauce. It occurred to me a long time ago that it would be great to dispense with the skewers altogether and just cook the chicken under the grill and add satay sauce, cucumber and noodles, so here's the recipe.

Mix the chicken with the garlic, 2 teaspoons of oil and the soy sauce. Stir well and set aside for 10 minutes.

Preheat the grill to medium-high. Mix together the sambal ingredients, adding enough water to make a spoonable sauce, and stir well.

Prepare the noodles according to the packet instructions and dress with a little oil and soy sauce. Cut the cucumber in half lengthways, remove the seeds and slice into 1cm semi-circles.

Brush the chicken lightly with oil and grill for 3–4 minutes on each side, or until cooked through. Divide the noodles between 4 bowls. Top with cucumber slices, the chicken, then the sambal. Decorate with the shredded spring onions and serve immediately.

Olive's chorizo tacos

SERVES 4 AS A SNACK, OR 2 AS A LIGHT SUPPER
1 tsp vegetable oil
100g diced chorizo
½ red onion, chopped
1 red or yellow pepper, deseeded and chopped
1 tsp ground cumin
1 tsp ground paprika
½ tsp chilli flakes
8 plain corn tortillas
200g soured cream, plus extra for serving
2 heaped tsp chipotle paste or chipotles en adobo (shop-bought or see p.294)
1 avocado, stoned and chopped
100g Cheddar cheese, grated
Handful of lettuce

I love the way my stepdaughter Olive makes simple suppers for herself. I recently asked her if she had any quick ideas – she was actually making some tacos at the time. She said, 'Is this any good?' And it seemed to me to be exactly what a simple supper should be all about. She doesn't care for spice that much, so the chilli flakes and chipotle paste or chipotles en adobo are my additions.

Warm the oil in a pan and add the chorizo, red onion, chopped pepper, cumin, paprika and chilli flakes. Cook for 3–5 minutes, stirring so the chorizo cooks evenly.

In another pan warm the tortillas for about 10 seconds on each side or microwave them all in a pile for 30 seconds. Mix the soured cream with the chipotle paste or the chipotles en adobo.

Fill the tortillas with the chorizo, avocado, cheese, soured cream and chipotle mixture and some lettuce.

Pork & broccoli stir-fry

SERVES 4
4 tbsp black bean sauce
2 tsp soy sauce
2 tbsp Chinese rice wine or dry sherry
½ tsp chilli flakes
Pinch of Chinese five-spice powder
2–4 tbsp vegetable or groundnut oil
2 large garlic cloves, sliced
20g root ginger, peeled and thinly sliced
400g pork tenderloin, cut on the diagonal into slices about 5mm thick
1 onion, sliced
1 red pepper, deseeded and sliced
300g tenderstem broccoli, cut into short pieces
400g fresh egg noodles
2 tsp cornflour, mixed with 60ml water
4 spring onions, sliced
Small handful of fresh coriander, roughly chopped

What everybody loves about this recipe are the flavours of black bean sauce, five-spice powder, Chinese rice wine and chilli. I like there to be a fair amount of sauce in the finished dish, but it does need to be silky and viscous – not too runny but not over reduced either, because then it won't coat the noodles pleasingly.

Mix together the black bean sauce, soy sauce, rice wine or sherry, chilli flakes and five-spice, then set aside.

Add a tablespoon of the oil to a wok and place over a high heat. Add the garlic and ginger and cook for 30 seconds.

Working in batches, add the slices of pork to the wok and fry until golden, then transfer to a plate.

Add a little more oil if needed, then add the onion, pepper and broccoli and stir-fry for a couple of minutes. Then add the pork, noodles, the black bean sauce mixture and the cornflour paste and cook for a minute until bubbling.

Take the wok off the heat, stir in the spring onions and coriander, then serve.

Lamb kebabs with flatbreads

SERVES 6
1kg lamb leg or shoulder, cut into bite-sized cubes
4 tbsp olive oil
3 tsp dried Greek oregano
1 lemon
Salt and black pepper

Toppings
4 tomatoes, thinly sliced
1 red onion, thinly sliced
½ small white cabbage or romaine lettuce, finely shredded
200g feta cheese, cubed
300g tzatziki (shop-bought or see p.291) or yoghurt

To serve
6 Greek flatbreads or large pitta breads, warmed or griddled

If possible, use Greek flatbreads (available frozen in some supermarkets) for this quick dish, but any pittas, flatbreads or flour tortillas will do. My flatbread recipe on page 301 is worth trying if you have time.

Heat a grill, griddle pan or barbecue to high.

Put the lamb in a bowl, add the olive oil and season with salt, pepper and 2 teaspoons of the oregano. Mix to coat the lamb, then thread the cubes on to skewers.

Grill for 3 or 4 minutes, then turn the skewers over and cook for about 3 minutes on the other side. Squeeze over some lemon juice and sprinkle with the rest of the oregano.

Push the meat off the skewers on to the flatbreads or pittas and add the toppings. Serve immediately.

FISH SUPPERS

It seems to me that the secret of getting people to really like fish dishes is to make them irresistible to eat, and also simple and quick, and that's what this chapter is all about.

To give you some examples, there's a smoked mackerel kedgeree (page 46), gnocchi with tomatoes, prawns and basil (page 53), and a baked bream dish with Spanish flavours of orange, pimentón and sherry (page 56) – the fish is baked in filleted form so that there are no bones to worry about. There's a seafood noodle soup with salmon (page 62), where thick slices of salmon are just dropped into the hot stock at the last minute, and finally a homage to the great skill we have with smoked fish on these islands: cullen skink (page 67), in which smoked haddock is cooked with creamy milk and floury potatoes; nothing complicated about that, but the dish is far greater than the sum of its parts.

I am completely aware that my access to really good fish is unusual, so for these recipes I've concentrated primarily on fish that you can buy in any supermarket. What's more, many of the dishes are for shellfish and smoked fish both of which, funnily enough, are probably more popular than fresh fish.

I could write chapters about the ethics of buying fish, the main theme being the debate on wild fish versus farmed. Wild fish are a diminishing resource, so if you're like me and believe that fish should be an important part of our diet, you realise that we have to eat some farmed fish. While salmon and single-portion sizes of bream or sea bass are normally going to be farmed and don't have the complexity of flavour of wild fish, they are still very nice to eat.

Also, not much in the way of wild fish is generally available in supermarkets, which is where many people buy their fish. I do know there is a lot of adverse publicity about fish farming, but I do still want to eat fish and

I believe there is a genuine wish to improve the methods used in aquaculture.

As far as cured fish is concerned, we do produce some really excellent smoked fish in this country, so it features in several of the recipes. Farmed mussels have been a great success and are completely sustainable, as are farmed clams, as you don't have to feed them anything – they live on plankton.

Prawns are the only other seafood ingredient in this chapter and the tip here is to buy the best you can afford. Don't worry about whether they're fresh or frozen; the majority of prawns you buy will have been frozen, as they simply don't keep in good condition for very long after being caught if not.

Smoked mackerel kedgeree

SERVES 4–6
350g basmati rice, rinsed
3 eggs
50g butter
2½ tsp garam masala
¼ tsp cayenne pepper
¼ tsp ground turmeric
150g frozen peas
140g smoked mackerel fillets, skinned and flaked
1 lemon
Small handful of parsley, chopped (optional)
Salt and black pepper

There's a good reason why oily fish like mackerel, salmon and herrings are cured and smoked – it preserves their freshness, albeit in a different form. You can keep a pack of hot smoked mackerel fillets in the fridge for ages. I couldn't possibly tell you how long I would keep them, but my wife is always trying to throw them out! This really excellent breakfast dish is equally good for supper and can be made largely from your store cupboard. The only fresh ingredient is parsley, which can be left out.

Put the rice in a pan with a teaspoon of salt and 530ml of water and bring to the boil over a high heat. Reduce the heat to low, cover the pan and simmer for 8–10 minutes until all the water has been absorbed and the rice is just tender.

After 8 minutes, check the rice by squeezing a grain between your fingers. You want rice that is soft on the outside, but still firm within. When the rice is ready, stir it gently with a fork to separate the grains.

Hard-boil the eggs for 8 minutes, then peel and cool. Cut the eggs into quarters.

Melt the butter in a heavy-based pan over a medium heat. Add the garam masala, cayenne and turmeric and fry for a minute, then add the hot rice and the peas and fry for 5 minutes. Season with salt and pepper. Gently fold in the mackerel, a squeeze of lemon juice and the eggs. Sprinkle with parsley, if using, then serve at once.

Smoked haddock rarebit with spinach

SERVES 2

2 x 120g pieces of undyed smoked haddock fillet
300g spinach, washed
Knob of butter
Salt and black pepper

Rarebit topping

80g strong Cheddar cheese, grated
1 tbsp beer
1 tbsp beaten egg
1 tsp Dijon mustard
Black pepper

I may be guilty of having too many smoked fish recipes in this book, but I do think we smoke fish particularly well in the UK. I came up with this recipe when thinking of the sort of dishes that me and my old chums delight in at my pub, The Cornish Arms. It's simply poached smoked haddock (you could also cook the fish very easily in a microwave), with a rarebit sauce like you would put on bread: cheese, beer, mustard and egg – all served on top of spinach. Lovely. Do go for undyed smoked haddock; the dyed stuff always tastes – well, dyed!

Put the smoked haddock fillets, skin-side down, in a pan and cover with cold water. Bring the water to the boil, allow it to bubble momentarily, then turn off the heat and leave the fish in the water to cook for 3–4 minutes. Remove with a slotted spoon and place on a baking sheet.

In a small bowl, mix the rarebit ingredients together and smooth the mixture over the haddock fillets. Grill them under a medium-high setting for a few minutes until they're golden and bubbling.

While the haddock is under the grill, wilt the spinach in a pan, stir in the butter and season with salt and pepper.

Divide the spinach between your plates and top with a piece of smoked haddock. If you want some carbs, serve on top of slices of buttered sourdough toast or with new potatoes.

Fear of fish

I've spent most of my life cooking fish and trying to persuade people to eat more of it. It's still a bit of a challenge to get most people enthused – what is it about fish that they don't like? The reality is that fish is incredibly easy and quick to cook, and generally doesn't require anything very complicated doing to it.

I think people don't think fish is interesting enough. I'm fond of quoting a couple of lines from Jane Grigson's *Fish Cookery*, published in 1973: 'I read a statement one day which struck me as particularly foolish. The writer remarked that fish could not be served as a main course when men were present, as they needed steak or some other red meat'. I can't help but feel that this attitude still prevails. I have to confess that even I love a small rib-eye steak from time to time, mainly because I'm currently addicted to a simple Bordeaux Supérieur called Château Maledan, which my son Charlie found for us all.

Then there are the little bones, the sliminess and the awful thought of eating the eyes. I know in my own family if I say I'm cooking fish tonight, I get replies such as, 'Actually, I'm not very hungry' or 'I've ordered a takeaway'. The objection can't really be the nutritive quantity of meat over fish because fish contains just as much protein and it's more easily digested. What is more, oily fish like herring, salmon and mackerel, contain masses of omega-3 fatty acids which are not only good for you but also an essential nutrient that must come from food, as the body cannot make it.

Maybe one of the reasons for this attitude to fish is that many of us were not brought up to eat fish regularly and therefore it's not part of our childhood memories or the aura of the comfort of home, which I think drives so much of what we do. The reason that I suspect this is the real answer is that in countries like Spain and Portugal, where people do eat much more fish than we do, they very often have fish dishes on high days and holidays, particularly Christmas Eve. I've sat down with a Spanish family for a Christmas festive dinner and while not being particularly enthused about the baked hake dish they were eating, I noted that they were really enjoying it with great merriment.

'The reality is that fish is incredibly easy and quick to cook, and generally doesn't require anything very complicated doing to it.'

In my last book *At Home*, I did say that Sas, while not relishing the idea of a simple fish supper, always loves it when I cook one. But the overriding reluctance and lack of enthusiasm for her is the smell of cooking fish at home and that may be the case for many other people. One of the reasons for this is that most extraction systems aren't particularly good. I know that in my kitchen in London we've got one of those charcoal filters with no extraction to the outside. It sort of works but I could still smell salmon on the top floor after cooking some the other day.

Another problem is that many of us don't have access to good enough fish. I'm not going to bore you with the reasons for it – I have done it so many times before. I will just say that if we were Spanish we'd all enjoy fabulous fresh fish as they do because we'd buy it so often. In the UK, fish doesn't sell quickly enough because we don't buy it enough. Vicious circle or what?

I remember a quote from one of my early books: 'Nothing is as exhilarating as fresh fish simply cooked'.

Gnocchi with tomatoes, prawns & basil

SERVES 4
400g raw prawns in the shell (defrosted if frozen)
40ml olive oil
1 garlic clove, finely chopped
250g cherry tomatoes, quartered
150ml chicken stock or water
600g gnocchi
Pinch of chilli flakes
Small handful of basil leaves, shredded
Salt and black pepper

Using a pack of ready-made gnocchi makes this a really quick supper. Peeling the prawns and making a stock with the shells takes a few moments but it's well worth it to extract every bit of their wonderful flavour.

Peel the prawns, cut the meat into small pieces and set aside. Put the heads and shells in a pan with half the oil, half the garlic and half the tomatoes, then fry gently for 3 minutes.

Add the chicken stock or water and boil until the liquid has reduced down to 4 or 5 tablespoons. Pass this through a sieve, taste and season, then set aside until ready to serve.

Cook the gnocchi in a pan of salted boiling water until they pop to the surface, then drain.

Heat the remaining olive oil in the pan and add the rest of the garlic and the chilli flakes, then the prawns and the remaining cherry tomatoes. Cook for a minute or so until the prawns are hot (and have turned pink), then stir in the gnocchi and the reserved sauce. Season with salt, pepper and shredded basil, then serve.

Mussels with garlic, chilli & lemon

SERVES 4
4 tbsp olive oil
2 garlic cloves, finely chopped
1½–2 red chillies, finely chopped
2kg live mussels, cleaned
Juice of 1 lemon
Handful of parsley, chopped (optional)

To serve
Crusty bread

This is a simplified version of a dish called hot shellfish, which we serve in many of our restaurants. It normally contains four or five different shellfish, like clams, cockles, oysters, small crabs or langoustines, but it's really nice just with mussels.

Put the olive oil, garlic and chillies in a small pan and cook gently for 1–2 minutes.

Heat a large pan, add the mussels and cover with a lid. Cook for 2–3 minutes, lifting the lid and stirring frequently until all the mussels have opened.

Strain the mussels in a colander over a bowl to catch the juices. Add 50ml of the juices to the pan of garlic and chillies, then stir in the lemon juice. Serve the mussels in large bowls with the garlic and chilli juices poured over them and sprinkle with parsley, if using. You'll need some crusty bread to mop up the juices.

Spanish bream with pimentón & sweety drop peppers

SERVES 6

60ml olive oil, plus extra for drizzling
1 onion, sliced
4 garlic cloves, sliced
1½ tsp pimentón
50ml sherry
350ml chicken stock
2 strips of orange zest (pared with a peeler)
650g waxy new potatoes, halved
50g sweety drop peppers, from a jar, drained
6 bream fillets, skinned and pin-boned
2 large tomatoes, sliced
Handful of flatleaf parsley, roughly chopped
Salt and black pepper

To serve
Aioli (see p.290)

TIP
If you don't have sweety drop peppers, you could chop up a couple of regular roasted peppers from a jar.

Much as I like whole fish with lovely Spanish flavours, I do find that dealing with the bones means I can't enjoy the accompaniments as much as I would like. Here, I cook all the vegetables first and then finish the dish with the fillets of bream on top. As we used to say in the Seafood Restaurant kitchen: 'it eats much better like this'. I'm very fond of sweety drop peppers – a cross between a cherry tomato and a jalapeño. They're sweet and tart and a bit spicy, but just have a rather silly name, I'm afraid. I prefer the South American name, biquinho peppers; even the other English name, Inca red drops, is better.

Heat the olive oil in a wide, shallow, flameproof casserole dish or a frying pan. Add the onion and garlic and cook for about 5 minutes until softened. Stir in the pimentón, then add the sherry.

Add the stock, orange zest and new potatoes and bring to the boil. Cover the pan and cook for 20–25 minutes until the potatoes are tender, then mix in the peppers.

Arrange the bream fillets over the potatoes and top with tomatoes. Drizzle over a little more olive oil, cover the pan with a lid, then cook for another 5–7 minutes. Season with salt and pepper and scatter over the parsley. Serve with aioli and perhaps a green salad.

Thai fishcakes with sweet chilli sauce

SERVES 2–4
AS A LIGHT MEAL

- 450g pollock fillet, or cod, haddock, hake or whiting, skinned
- 1 tbsp nam pla (Thai fish sauce)
- 1½ tbsp red Thai curry paste (I like Aroy-D, Mae Ploy and Namjai brands)
- 1 lemongrass stalk, roughly chopped
- Small handful of coriander, roughly chopped
- 1 egg
- 1 tsp sugar
- ½ tsp salt
- 50g French beans, thinly sliced into rounds
- Oil, for frying

To serve

- Thai sweet chilli sauce mixed with 1–2 tbsp white wine vinegar

This is a great way of turning quite bland white fish into something that tastes wonderful and is also very easy to make. You just blitz everything in a food processor, roll the mixture into balls and fry. I also think these go well with a shop-bought sauce, such as my favourite 'Healthy Boy' brand, which has a label showing a baby holding a bottle of sauce and looking very happy.

Put all the fishcake ingredients, except the French beans and the oil, in a food processor and pulse until smooth. Stir in the green beans.

Divide the mixture into 16, roll into balls, then flatten them between your palms. Add some oil to a pan to a depth of about 1cm and heat. To check if the oil is hot enough, add a small piece of bread to the pan – if it browns and sizzles on the surface, the oil is ready.

Fry the fishcakes in batches for a minute on each side until golden brown. Drain on kitchen paper and serve with the sweet chilli sauce.

Prawn & fennel risotto

SERVES 4
1 tbsp oil
350g raw prawns in the shell, defrosted if frozen
1.25 litres chicken stock
½ tsp fennel seeds, lightly crushed
30g unsalted butter
2 shallots, chopped
1 fennel bulb, finely chopped
1 garlic clove, chopped
250g risotto rice, such as Arborio
120ml dry white wine
30g Parmesan, grated, plus extra for serving
Chives, chopped
Salt and black pepper

In the interests of keeping things simple, I tried to write a recipe for prawn risotto in which I added cooked prawns at the end, but it didn't work for me; you need the flavour from the shells. So, I've made the stock absolutely basic, just adding the shells to chicken stock and simmering them for a bit. This recipe was inspired by a conversation I had with Matt Tebbutt at the restaurant Bocca di Lupo in Soho. The debate about whether or not to add cheese to seafood risottos came up. Matt pointed out that the previous year, chefs from Trattoria al Gatto Nero on the island of Burano in the Venice lagoon came over to cook at the Dartmouth Food Festival. Their risotto, using seafood from the Venice lagoon, contained plenty of Parmesan.

Heat the oil in a pan and fry the prawns for 3–4 minutes until pink. When the prawns are cool enough to handle, remove the heads and shells to use in the stock. Cut each prawn into 3 pieces and set them aside for later.

Heat the stock in a pan and add the prawn heads and shells and the fennel seeds. Simmer for 10–15 minutes, then pass everything through a sieve into a clean pan, pressing the heads and shells to extract as much flavour as possible.

Melt half the butter in a heavy-based pan then add the shallots, fennel and garlic and fry gently until softened. Add the rice and stir for a couple of minutes until it's well-coated with butter, then add the white wine and allow it to boil and bubble up.

Add the hot stock a ladleful at a time, stirring frequently until each addition is absorbed before adding the next. Keep stirring until the stock is almost completely absorbed. When the rice is just tender but still firm to the bite (al dente), stir in the prawns over a low heat until they are heated through. Stir in the Parmesan and the rest of the butter, then garnish with chives and extra Parmesan and serve at once.

Crispy-skinned salmon with cucumber, apple & dill salad

SERVES 4
1 cucumber, finely sliced
1 crisp apple, finely sliced
1 red onion, very finely sliced
Handful of dill, roughly chopped
125g (8 tbsp) crème fraiche
Squeeze of lemon juice
4 x 120g salmon fillets
Oil, for brushing
Salt and black pepper

To serve
New potatoes
Mint sprigs
Butter

Being an oily fish, salmon lends itself to being cooked so the skin is crisp. The method is simple: cook the fish skin- side down for most of its cooking time, then turn it over for just a minute or so. Aim to leave the centre of the fillets slightly undercooked. A temperature probe is very useful for this sort of cooking, and for this should ideally read 55–60°C in the centre of the fish.

Cook the potatoes in a pan of salted water, preferably with a few sprigs of fresh mint, until tender. Add a knob of butter, set aside and keep warm.

Mix the cucumber, apple, onion, dill, crème fraiche and lemon juice in a bowl. Season with salt and pepper and stir well to combine.

Brush the salmon fillets with oil and season with salt and pepper. Cook them, skin-side down, over a medium heat for 4 minutes, then turn them over and cook the other side for 1–2 minutes only.

Serve the salmon with the salad and new potatoes.

Seafood noodle soup with pak choi

SERVES 4
200g pak choi
250g flat rice noodles
75g cooked, peeled prawns, each cut in half lengthways
150g salmon fillet, very thinly sliced
1 red chilli, sliced
2 spring onions, sliced diagonally
Handful of mint leaves
Handful of coriander leaves
1 lime, cut into wedges

Soup base
1.2 litres chicken stock
3 garlic cloves, bruised
1 red chilli, halved
15g root ginger, peeled and sliced
2 star anise
3 tbsp nam pla (Thai fish sauce)
2 tbsp soy sauce

To serve
Soy sauce
Chilli sauce

This is a rendition of pho, the famous Vietnamese dish. To simplify it for a quick supper, I use bought chicken stock but add traditional Vietnamese flavourings and then some reasonably inexpensive seafood at the last minute. The secret of success is to add the salmon seconds before serving, so it's barely cooked and very juicy and tender.

Put all the soup base ingredients in a large pan and simmer for 25–30 minutes. Turn off the heat, remove the garlic, chilli ginger and star anise with a slotted spoon and discard them.

Trim the pak choi and cut them in half through the bulb or into quarters if large. Cook the rice noodles according to the packet instructions and drain them.

Add the pak choi to the stock, cook for 2 minutes, then add the prawns and salmon. Cook for 1 minute.

Divide the cooked noodles between 4 bowls, top with the salmon, prawns and pak choi and ladle over the stock. Top each bowl with slices of chilli, spring onions, herbs and a lime wedge.

Serve with soy sauce and chilli sauce at the table.

Garlic & chilli prawns on puréed butter beans

SERVES 2

Butter beans
1 tbsp olive oil
1 garlic clove, chopped
400g tin of butter beans, drained
Juice of ½ lemon
Salt and black pepper

Prawns
2 garlic cloves, peeled
Handful of flatleaf parsley leaves, chopped
50ml olive oil
¼ tsp crushed chilli flakes
225g peeled, raw prawns

One of the revelations for me when thinking of simple dishes was taking a tin of, say, lentils, black beans, chickpeas or butter beans, puréeing them and then adding flavours in the same way as when making mashed potatoes. For instance, olive oil, garlic and lemon juice as in this recipe, or butter, a little cream and spring onions, or indeed harissa or Parmesan. For this dish I have added lovely garlicky prawns on top of the butter beans.

Warm the oil for the butter beans in a pan and add the garlic. Cook for a minute, then add the beans and cook for 3–4 minutes until warmed through. Add a couple of tablespoons of water and the lemon juice, then blend to form a purée in a blender or food processor.

Season the purée with salt and pepper and keep it warm while you cook the prawns. Add a little more water if you need to adjust the consistency.

For the prawns, chop the garlic together with the parsley to form a coarse paste. Pour the oil into a wide pan and when it's hot, add the chilli flakes and the garlic mixture and cook over a gentle heat for a minute until sizzling and fragrant. Increase the heat a little, then add the prawns and stir-fry for 2–3 minutes.

Serve the purée topped with the prawns and oil and have some crusty bread on the side to mop the juices.

Cullen skink

SERVES 4
50g butter
1 onion, finely chopped
1.2 litres whole milk
750g floury potatoes, such as Maris Piper or King Edward, peeled and diced
450g undyed smoked haddock fillet
2 tbsp chopped parsley, plus a little extra to garnish
Salt and black pepper

We included this soup in my third Cornwall series as a hearty meal to come home to after a day out at sea. Very similar to New England fish chowder, it's a perfectly apt combination of the good things grown in the gardens of Cullen on the Moray Firth on the east coast of Scotland – potatoes, sweet mild onions and parsley – coupled with smoked local haddock and full-fat milk.

Melt the butter in a pan, add the onion and cook gently for 7–8 minutes, until it's soft but not browned. Pour in the milk and bring it to the boil. Add the diced potatoes and simmer for 20 minutes, until they are very soft.

Add the smoked haddock and simmer for 3–4 minutes, until it's cooked and flakes easily. Carefully lift the fish out and place it on a plate, then leave it to cool slightly. Meanwhile, crush some of the cooked potatoes against the side of the pan with a wooden spoon to thicken the soup a little.

When the smoked haddock is cool enough to handle, break it into flakes, discarding the skin and any bones. Put it backin the pan, stir in the parsley and season to taste. Serve garnished with a little more chopped parsley.

Poached hake with a parsley & chive sauce

SERVES 2
2 x 160g pieces of hake fillet, skinned
300ml whole milk
1 egg yolk
1 tbsp cornflour
Large handful of curly parsley, chopped
8–10 chives, finely chopped
Salt and black pepper

To serve
Mashed potatoes

Are you old enough to remember frozen cod and parsley sauce, which came in a little pouch? It wasn't half bad but the memory did rather put me off considering it as a dish for my restaurant until the mid nineties, when I tried using fresh cod in my own home-made parsley sauce and discovered how great it was. Essentially, this is just a slightly jazzed-up version of those pouches; the chives are particularly lovely with the parsley.

Put the hake and milk in a saucepan just large enough to hold the fish and poach for 3–4 minutes until just cooked through. Carefully lift the fish out and keep it warm. If the fish has the skin on, peel it off at this stage.

Mix the egg yolk and cornflour together in a bowl, add a ladleful of the warm poaching milk and whisk until smooth. Add this mixture to the pan of milk and cook over a low-medium heat until thickened. Season with salt and pepper and stir in the chopped herbs.

Serve the fish with the sauce spooned over the top and some mash. Some peas or greens make a good accompaniment.

Warm sole salad

SERVES 2
2 tbsp semolina
160g small sole fillets, cut in half
50–60ml olive oil, for frying
Salt and black pepper

Salad
1 tomato, cut into thin wedges
½ romaine or cos lettuce, leaves torn
1 small avocado, stoned and sliced
4 basil leaves, torn

Dressing
3 tbsp sunflower oil
1 tbsp mild olive oil
1 tbsp red wine vinegar
½ tsp salt
¼ tsp sugar

When people ask me for a simple fish dish, I just say, 'Fish and salad' and this is it.

Put the semolina on a plate. Season the sole fillets with salt and pepper and then turn them in the semolina to lightly coat. Heat the olive oil in a frying pan over a moderate heat. Shallow fry the sole fillets for a couple of minutes until lightly golden and just cooked through.

While the sole is cooking, make the salad. Sprinkle the tomato wedges with salt and leave for 2 minutes, then place them with the rest of the salad ingredients in a bowl. Whisk together the dressing ingredients.

Tuck the pieces of warm sole into the salad and dress with some of the dressing. Serve immediately with the rest of the dressing on the side.

Freddy Parker Bowles's chalk stream trout with egg-fried rice

SERVES 4

- 4 x 100–150g chalk stream trout fillets
- 2 tbsp olive oil
- 2 tbsp soy sauce
- Juice of ½ lemon
- 10g root ginger, grated
- 4 spring onions, thinly sliced

Egg-fried rice

- 4 spring onions
- 2 tbsp olive or vegetable oil
- 3 eggs, beaten
- 400g cooked long-grain rice (about 140g uncooked)
- 1 tbsp soy sauce

This recipe came about because I mentioned to Sas that I wanted recipes from mothers who were trying to cook something a little different for their darlings. 'Ring Sara', she said, 'she's bound to be cooking something special, particularly if Tom has anything to do with it'. What I like about this is that it's very simple and doesn't try too hard to introduce teenagers to something a bit adventurous. She came up with it because her son Freddy loves soy sauce, and her daughter Lola loves rice. She was rather apologetic about insisting on chalk stream trout, but the recipe also works very well with supermarket trout fillets, although the pedigree isn't quite the same! Incidentally, baking fish in foil in the oven is one of the simplest ways of cooking it well. Sara's family love this trout with egg-fried rice, but you could also serve it with plain steamed rice.

Preheat the oven to 200°C/Fan 180°C. Lay 2 of the fillets, skin-side down, on a piece of foil measuring about 30 x 50cm. Lift up the edges of the foil to stop the liquid running off and sprinkle over the olive oil, soy sauce, lemon juice, ginger and spring onions. Place the other 2 fillets, skin-side up, on top.

Fold the foil into a loose parcel and bake in the oven for 10–12 minutes. Unwrap and put the fillets in a warm serving dish, then pour the contents of the foil parcel over the fish.

While the trout is cooking, prepare the rice. Slice the spring onions, separating the green parts from the white. Heat the oil in a wok or frying pan, add the white parts of the spring onions and let them soften for a minute or so.

Add the beaten eggs, then stir and cook for another minute until the eggs are almost fully scrambled. Pour in the rice and stir until the grains separate. Add the green parts of the onions and the soy sauce and stir until everything is well combined. Serve with the trout.

Clams with garlic, olive oil, coriander & chilli

SERVES 4
60ml olive oil
4 garlic cloves, sliced
1kg carpet shell clams
⅛ tsp chilli flakes
Splash of white wine
30g butter
Handful of fresh coriander, roughly chopped
Black pepper

To serve
Crusty bread

I don't know how I missed this dish on previous trips to Portugal, but I ate it at a restaurant called Cervejaria Ramiro in Lisbon last November. It's an amazingly simple dish, made unusual and remarkable by the use of chilli and coriander. It's best with clams or you can use mussels or cockles, but they do have to be raw.

Heat the olive oil gently in a pan, add the garlic and cook for 2–3 minutes over a moderate heat until soft.

Wash the clams in plenty of cold water, swirling them around with your hands to remove as much grit as possible.

Add the clams, chilli flakes and wine to the pan, cover with a lid and bring to the boil over a high heat. Then lower the heat for a couple of minutes to allow the clams to steam open.

Tip everything into a colander or sieve over a bowl and transfer the clams to a warm serving dish. Taste the juice and if it's really salty, spoon off half of it and discard; if it tastes good, use all of it.

Pour the juice back into the pan and place the pan over the heat. Add the butter and reduce the liquid by about three-quarters. Stir in the coriander, season with black pepper, then pour over the clams. Serve with lots of crusty bread.

Haddock fillets with spring onions, red pepper & lemon juice

SERVES 2

- 2 haddock fillets (skin on), each about 160g
- 1 tbsp plain flour
- 50ml olive oil
- 2 spring onions, thinly sliced
- ½ roasted red pepper, from a jar, cut into 1cm dice
- Juice of ½ lemon
- ½ tsp soy sauce
- Salt and black pepper

As I have mentioned in the introduction to this book, this dish was my first taste of hospital food during a recent stay, and at the time I thought that there could be no better diet for a patient. Things didn't turn out quite like that subsequently, but this is a celebration of how food could, or should be, in hospital in a perfect world.

Season the fish fillets with salt and pepper and then lightly dust with flour.

Heat 2 tablespoons of the olive oil in a large non-stick frying pan and gently fry the fish over a low-medium heat for about 2–3 minutes on each side. Transfer the fish to a plate and cover with foil to keep it warm.

Add the remaining oil to the pan and add the spring onions, red pepper, lemon juice and soy sauce. Stir together until warmed through, then serve the fish immediately with the sauce spooned over the top.

ONE-POT SUPPERS

The flamboyant TV cook Keith Floyd used to love one-pot meals. David Pritchard, the director with whom I worked for twenty-five years and who also directed most of Keith's best-loved programmes, used to say that the great appeal of one-pot dishes for Keith was that he liked going to the pub possibly more than doing TV and one pots allowed you to do both.

They'd start filming in the morning with a dish like the beef stifado on page 110. Keith would brown batches of beef in olive oil, add onions and sugar, cook gently, then add garlic, cinnamon sticks, cloves and star anise. He'd pour in some vinegar, red wine and tinned tomatoes, add salt and pepper and cover the dish with a lid, then put it in a medium oven for an hour or so. Then he'd go off to the pub for a pint. By the time he came back, the meat was tender and starting to fall apart, ready to serve with orzo pasta. Job done, filming finished, time for lunch. David liked them too because he only had to concentrate on the one pot.

Personally, I love one-pot dishes and to me they feel like the very essence of simple suppers. Being naturally inclined to disorder – my wife often calls me 'Captain Chaos' – the knowledge that I've planned everything and put it into a slow cooker in the morning fills me with enormous satisfaction that I could have been so well organised. Even people who are naturally disorganised are in control sometimes.

Mentioning my wife reminds me that the other good thing about single-pan dishes is keeping clutter out of the kitchen. In a restaurant kitchen, whatever pan you use on the stove you fling into a large wheelie bin for the kitchen porters to take away and wash, while occasionally muttering under their breath about the chef's profligacy. I'm ashamed to admit that with my restaurant background I've been guilty in the past of using too many pans at home. But no longer, because there's been a lot of moaning about the washing up. I do the cooking, they do the clearing up, so one-pot meals keep everyone happy.

Surveying the recipes in this chapter I can't help but say they're all perfect examples of the one-pot genre. May I draw your attention, however, to a couple of them. First of all to kapuska (page 107). The name rhymes charmingly with babuska – making me think of Kate Bush – and in Ukraine refers to a headscarf and an old woman, or to grandmother in Russian. This fabulous cabbage dish is a staple of many poorer people of Eastern Europe and transforms the humble cabbage into something noble. And like polenta it's one of those dishes that absolutely everyone loves. By the way, you don't have to use meat mince. It's very nice made with a good vegan alternative.

Another favourite of mine, and a dish you can knock up very quickly in one pan, is chicken, chorizo and prawn jambalaya (page 94): prawns and rice and what Creoles call the holy trinity – green peppers, celery and onions.

Wild garlic, broad bean & leek risotto

SERVES 4

300g podded broad beans, fresh or frozen and defrosted
60g butter
1 leek, trimmed, halved lengthways and finely sliced
300g Arborio rice
100ml white wine
1–1.2 litres hot vegetable stock
Handful of wild garlic, washed and chopped (or 3 garlic cloves, chopped, and a handful of flatleaf parsley)
60g Parmesan, grated
Salt and black pepper

TIP

If you're using chopped garlic cloves and parsley instead of wild garlic, add the chopped garlic with the leek, and the parsley just before the Parmesan.

A little obsession of mine: I don't think there are enough recipes for broad beans in this world. I love them, but unless the beans are incredibly young and tender you do have to, what I call, double-pod them for this dish – that is, remove the grey outer skin of each bean. That's a good reason for going out and finding the first tender beans of the season. As I write this, I'm thinking that the evenings are getting lighter and it's nearly time for wild garlic, which goes so well with broad beans. Don't you just love the seasons?

Remove the greyish outer skins from the beans – you should have about 200g after doing this.

Melt half the butter in a large pan and add the leek. Sweat for about 3–4 minutes until soft, then add the rice and stir. Once the rice is all coated in buttery leeks, add the white wine and allow it to boil and bubble up.

Add the hot stock a ladleful at a time, stirring frequently until each addition is absorbed before adding the next. Continue until you have only a couple of ladlefuls left, then stir in the broad beans and add the remaining stock.

Take the pan off the heat and stir in the wild garlic, three-quarters of the grated Parmesan and the rest of the butter. Stir until well combined then season with salt and pepper. Serve with the remaining Parmesan.

Pea & potato soup with horseradish

SERVES 4
120g butter
1 onion, chopped
50ml white wine
200g potatoes, chopped
1 litre chicken or
vegetable stock
500g frozen peas
1 tsp creamed horseradish
1 tsp salt
60g natural yoghurt,
plus a little extra to
serve mixed with more
horseradish if you like

Everyone loves pea soup. My memory of my mother's pea soup is how green it was and this was because she added half the peas right at the end of the cooking time. The horseradish is hardly noticeable in the soup, but it's one of those situations where if it wasn't there, you would notice its absence. I've also included the option of some extra horseradish stirred into the yoghurt to add to the soup as you serve it. You might also like to add some grated horseradish as in the photo opposite – our food stylist, Aya Nishimura, got a little over enthusiastic!

Melt the butter in a pan, add the onion and soften over a medium heat for 5–10 minutes.

Add the white wine, potato, stock and half the peas, then simmer for 20–25 minutes until everything is very soft.

Add the remaining peas, horseradish and salt, then cook for another 5 minutes or so. Add the yoghurt and blend the soup until smooth. (If you want a really smooth texture you could also pass the soup through a sieve.)

Serve with an extra teaspoon of yoghurt and a little horseradish swirled into each bowl if desired.

Tomato bread soup

SERVES 4
100ml olive oil
4 garlic cloves, chopped
700ml passata
200g stale ciabatta or sourdough white bread, torn into chunks
Salt and black pepper

To serve
50g Parmesan, grated
A few torn basil leaves
Extra virgin olive oil, to drizzle
Flaked sea salt

This is one of those great Italian recipes for using up stale bread. I've called it a soup, but the Italian name, pappa al pomodoro, means tomato pap or baby food. When my three boys were babies, I always meant to purée lots of lovely things like tomatoes, bread, olive oil and garlic, but never got around to it. The theory with me then was that you need to set children off on the right road, food wise, even when they're tiny babies. Personally, I make much more sourdough than we can use and much as I like very crisp toast, the bread comes into its own in this dish or in the panzanella on page 144.

Warm the olive oil in a pan over a medium heat and add the garlic. Soften the garlic for a minute, then stir in the passata and add 800ml of water. Season with a teaspoon of salt and some black pepper.

Bring to the boil, then turn the heat down to a simmer and stir in the torn chunks of bread. Cook for 15 minutes until the bread is falling apart and the soup has thickened. Mash with a potato masher if the bread remains chunky.

Check the seasoning and serve with grated Parmesan, basil leaves and a drizzle of extra virgin olive oil. I like to offer a bowl of sea salt flakes, too.

Coconut prawn curry
Chingri malai

SERVES 4

4 medium onions, peeled, 2 roughly chopped and 2 finely sliced
25ml vegetable or sunflower oil
3cm cinnamon stick
½ tsp garam masala
½ tsp ground turmeric
½ tsp mild chilli powder
15g root ginger, finely grated
3 garlic cloves, grated
300g large peeled raw prawns
280ml coconut milk
1 tsp salt
1 tsp sugar

To serve
Basmati rice

My book on Indian cookery had the strapline: 'in search of the perfect curry'. This recipe was certainly in my top ten and is simple to boot. Called chingri malai, this dish is from Rakhi Dasgupta's famous restaurant Kewpies in Kolkata, and is one of her signature dishes.

Blend the 2 roughly chopped onions in a mini food processor to make a fine paste, adding a splash of water if needed.

Heat the oil in a wide heavy-based saucepan over a medium heat. Add the cinnamon stick and fry for a minute until fragrant. Add the sliced onions and fry for 10 minutes until golden, then stir in the garam masala, turmeric and chilli powder and fry for 30 seconds. Add the onion paste, ginger and garlic, then fry for 5 minutes or until the onion paste is golden. Stir often, adding a splash of water if the mixture catches on the bottom of the pan.

Stir in the prawns, cook them for just 1 minute, then pour in the coconut milk, salt, sugar and 75ml of water. Bring to a simmer and cook for 5 minutes or until the sauce has reduced by half and the prawns are pink and cooked through. Serve with basmati rice.

John Harris

I might be accused of rambling a little in this book about light-hearted cooking – that is, cooking delicious things without a lot of fanfare and fuss. But I have in the back of my mind a volume that my parents cherished called the *Weekend Book*, which came from a time before television and the internet; a time when books could exist simply to entertain. I've mentioned this treasure before and here is what I said about it in my book *Long Weekends*.

'The book had sections on early morning bird calls, indoor and outdoor games, maps of the summer stars, poetry, songs with the musical score for piano accompaniment, dance steps with little black and white footprints, and weekend recipes, which were introduced with the advice, "weekend cookery should be either very quick, a good meal produced in half an hour, or very slow, to put on before you go to tennis or to lazing".'

The point is that I don't just want to write a book full of recipes. I want to try to entertain you as well and I'm thinking of a couple of female friends of mine who like to read cookery books before going to sleep. So it is with no more preamble that I want to tell you more about my friend John Harris.

If you have watched any of my three television series on Cornwall you'll know how very popular a guest John Harris has proved to be. John has been head gardener at Tresillian House, just outside Newquay, since 1984 and I first met him when we were filming an episode for the first series in the orchard he planned and planted in the 1970s. In the next series I came across him in the kitchen garden which he looks after at the same house, and in the third series he came over to my summer house kitchen at my cottage in Padstow to talk about cider among other things, and to taste a dish that I created in his honour – the gratin of chicken, leek and cider on page 227.

Talking to him about cider making and threshing corn was a step back in time that I very much enjoyed. When I was a child living on our farm in Oxfordshire at a time before combine harvesters, our corn was cut and gathered into sheaves, collected in stooks in the fields, then picked up on a tractor and trailer and stored in our Dutch barn.

'The point is that I don't just want to write a book full of recipes. I want to try to entertain you as well.'

A pink threshing machine and hay baler would then arrive in the autumn and thresh the grain – remove the corn from the stalks and husks. It was a time of great excitement for me, as when the stack of sheaves got near to the bottom a flurry of rats would escape to be chased by the farm dogs and me. The farmhand's Jack Russells dispatched them with consummate skill. I've never forgotten the squeals.

We talked about John's threshing days when he was young and about the lunches of cider and sandwiches they'd all have while sitting on corn sacks. The older men would try to get the youngsters like John drunk, saying, 'E're boy, 'ave another'. All this took me back to a time when farm life was filled with characters and humour. John seems like someone from a bygone past that simply doesn't exist any more, but we all wish it did. He has not been well of late and as he walked through the kitchen door I asked him how he was. He replied, 'Fair to middlin'', but what is so amazing about him is his contentedness and lack of ego. During our conversation he mentioned, just in passing, that his latest book, *The Natural Gardener,* had sold 17,000 copies in the United States. In these days when everybody, including myself, is on the internet talking about how we've done this and that, I found his modesty so refreshing.

I bought a copy of *The Natural Gardener: A Guide to the Ancient Practice of Moon Gardening*. In addition to detail about gardening by the phases of the moon, there's lots of great information about how he restored the kitchen gardens at Tresillian House and designed and planted the apple orchard near where we filmed. John turned out to be a naturally good writer and here are a couple of paragraphs which I found very amusing, to give you a flavour of the book:

'It was 1990 that the estate was visited by Mrs Thatcher, it was a big occasion for us, and everyone was there for the event. The idea was for us to line up, have a polite word and move on. I was last in the queue, but when it came to my turn we just started chatting. Whatever your political take on her was, Margaret Thatcher was famous for her presence close up. When she spoke to you, she made you feel important. Very powerful people seem to have this trait in common.

She asked me about my work at Tresillian. (She'd been well briefed and seemed to know more about me than I did myself.) Then we started talking in depth about gardening and her favourite plants and how she found the garden in No. 10 very relaxing – a place where she could walk in peace and clear her head.

As we stood there blathering, it became obvious that her entourage expected me to move on and her to be somewhere else more important. But we kept chatting away for about 20 minutes until an aide stepped in and said, "Prime Minister we really must be –"

"Don't interrupt!" The sudden ferocity of her voice sent the aide scuttling away. Mrs Thatcher turned back to me and said, "I want you to do our garden at No. 10, I'll be in touch".

Six weeks later she was kicked out and I was never asked again. Maybe Mr Major got his peas from Tesco.'

While we were filming, John asked me to have a go at water dowsing with him and I have to say I was a little reluctant about it at first. In the same way, I've always found getting involved with conjurers a bit awkward because I really don't want to see how the magic is done, but since I was being filmed I agreed. Water dowsing is described on the internet as a pseudoscience, but I discovered the lie of a freshwater pipe under the ground – just two bent bits of microbore copper pipe. It worked not only for me but also for the rest of the crew, except for Chris the cameraman.

John has found water for hundreds of people over his lifetime, but he knows dowsing doesn't work for everyone. He told me that there is a young woman working for him in the garden at the moment who can't do water dowsing to save her life.

John seems to have a feeling for water. His books on moon or lunar gardening describe a method of gardening that's governed by the phases of the moon, an idea that has been around for thousands of years. The theory is that just as the moon exerts a gravitational pull on the oceans, it does the same to the water table lying just under the ground. I've looked up the science of this and generally found it quite baffling, but the point is that this theory has worked for John and his gardens. If water divining works, why shouldn't lunar gardening work too?

During our many conversations, John has repeatedly mentioned the importance of the knowledge of our ancestors and how the old ways have been overtaken by the inventions of modern life, such as supermarkets and the internet. At the age of eight-three he has published eight books but says he's still got lots to do. He's planning on giving writing about gardening a rest for a while and his next book is going to be about poetry. I'm looking forward to it.

'John seems like someone from a bygone past that simply doesn't exist any more, but we all wish it did.'

Green rice with garlic, parsley & mussels
Arroz verde

SERVES 4–5
60ml olive oil
60g shallots, finely chopped
12 garlic cloves, finely chopped
1 litre chicken stock
100g flatleaf parsley, chopped
1½ tsp salt
400g short-grain paella rice
500g raw mussels, scrubbed
Juice of ½ lemon

To serve
Aioli (I like the Chovi brand available in supermarkets or see p.290)

I love these Spanish paella-type dishes. There's a similar, but slightly more complicated and expensive version of this recipe in my book Long Weekends. *I remember filming it at a restaurant on the beach in Cádiz. I chose the arroz verde, but the crew went for seafood paella coloured with the extremely bright yellow of fake saffron. The camera pulled away from my demure green and white bowl to reveal everybody else wearing sunglasses while eating.*

Heat the olive oil in a shallow flameproof casserole dish over a medium heat. Add the shallots and garlic, then fry gently for 5 minutes until soft. Stir in the stock, parsley and salt and bring to the boil.

Sprinkle in the rice, stir once, then leave to simmer vigorously over a medium-high heat for 6 minutes. Put the mussels on top and shake the pan briefly so that they sink into the rice slightly. Lower the heat and leave to simmer gently for another 12 minutes.

At the end of the cooking time, almost all the liquid should have been absorbed, the mussels opened and the rice will be pitted with small holes. Squeeze over the lemon juice and serve with the aioli.

Chicken, chorizo & prawn jambalaya

SERVES 6
4 tbsp sunflower oil
100g chorizo, diced
2 tsp pimentón
8 garlic cloves, chopped
1 onion, chopped
2 green peppers, deseeded and chopped
4 celery sticks, sliced
2 red chillies, sliced
½ tsp dried oregano
2 skinless, boneless chicken breasts, cut into bite-sized pieces
12 raw peeled prawns
450g long-grain rice
750ml chicken stock
3 spring onions, trimmed, thinly sliced
Salt and black pepper

To serve
Tabasco sauce
Lemon wedges

The origins of jambalaya were probably a paella-type dish from Southwest France and Catalan Spain, but with what was available locally in Louisiana rather than olive oil and saffron. The combination of green peppers, celery and onions is known as the 'holy trinity' and is the flavour that most typifies Creole cookery. I use chorizo and paprika in this, but you could use a smoked Polish sausage instead.

Heat the oil in a large, deep frying pan, add the chorizo and fry until lightly browned. Add the pimentón, garlic, onion, peppers, celery, chillies and oregano, then cook over a medium heat until softened.

Add the chicken and fry for 2 minutes, then add the prawns and rice and stir for 1 minute.

Pour in the chicken stock and season with salt and pepper, then bring to the boil. Cover the pan with a lid and simmer gently for about 8 minutes. Add the prawns, cover again and simmer for about another 4 minutes, until the rice is tender and has absorbed the liquid.

Stir in the spring onions and serve with Tabasco sauce and lemon wedges.

Summer chicken soup with tomato & tarragon

SERVES 4–6
2 tbsp olive oil
4 spring onions, sliced on the diagonal
2 celery sticks, finely sliced
1.5 litres good chicken stock
8 new potatoes, peeled and diced
2 skinless chicken breasts
4 small carrots, peeled and sliced
2 small courgettes, sliced
8 cherry tomatoes, quartered
150g peas, fresh or frozen
Small handful of tarragon and/or parsley, chopped
Salt and black pepper

I have fond memories of the chicken soups my dad used to make at our farm in the Cotswolds when I was young. Mine is a bit more seasonal than his was, but the basis is the same – good chicken stock. Use a really good supermarket stock for this or it might be worth investing a bit of time making your own from my recipe on page 305.

Heat the oil in a pan, add the spring onions and celery and fry gently for a few minutes. Add the stock and potatoes, then bring to the boil. Cover the pan with a lid, turn down the heat and simmer gently for 10 minutes.

Slice the chicken breasts in half lengthways and then cut them into small chunks. Add the chicken to the pan with the carrots, courgettes, tomatoes and peas and continue to simmer for 5–10 minutes.

Taste and season with salt and pepper and add the tarragon and/or parsley before serving.

Spanish omelette

SERVES 4
75ml olive oil
400g potatoes, peeled and thinly sliced
1 small onion, finely sliced
8 large eggs, beaten
Small handful of flatleaf parsley, chopped
160g roasted red peppers, from a jar (drained weight), sliced into slivers, to garnish
Salt and black pepper

To serve
Green salad

You'll need a non-stick frying pan about 24cm in diameter.

If there's ever a dish that sums up a simple supper it's a Spanish omelette. It's the sort of thing I might make after coming back from the pub or from surfing or being out on the boat. I like the simple mixture of protein (eggs) and carbohydrates (potatoes) and making it is just fun. It's a bit like the scene at the end of the film 'Big Night' with Stanley Tucci and Tony Shalhoub when their restaurant is folding and they make a classic omelette to cheer themselves up. There are certain dishes that are deeply therapeutic as well as absolutely bound to make you smile.

Heat most of the oil in the pan over a low-medium heat. Add the potatoes and onion and fry gently for 10–15 minutes, without allowing them to brown.

Season the eggs with salt and plenty of pepper, then add the chopped parsley. Pour the mixture over the potato and onion slices in the pan and stir very gently to combine. Leave to cook over a low heat for about 7–8 minutes until almost set and the underside of the omelette is golden when lifted gently with a spatula.

Carefully slide the omelette on to a plate. Add the rest of the oil to the pan, then return the omelette to the pan, cooked side up, and cook for another minute or so.

Turn the omelette out on to a serving dish and cut it into wedges. Garnish with slivers of roasted red peppers and serve with a green salad.

Prawn dumplings with vinegar & soy dipping sauce

SERVES 2

10 prawn dumplings, aka har gow or dim sum (available online and in supermarkets)

Dipping sauce

1 tbsp Chinese black vinegar
1 tbsp soy sauce
1 tsp toasted sesame oil
⅛–¼ tsp chilli flakes

Asian slaw

A wedge of red or white cabbage
1 carrot, peeled and grated
Small handful of bean sprouts
1 spring onion, finely sliced
Small handful of coriander, chopped
Small handful of mint, chopped
¼ tsp chilli flakes
Good pinch of sesame seeds

Slaw dressing

1 tsp soy sauce
1 tsp toasted sesame oil
1 tsp Chinese black vinegar
½ tsp honey

In Cremorne, on the north side of the Harbour Bridge in Sydney, there's a small Chinese dumpling restaurant called Fang. A great aspect of life in that fair city are the myriad places where you can go to get something good to eat – not a posh restaurant, just a place down the road. Fang has a little kitchen, open to the public, where two or three girls make dumplings. I think seeing them make these dumplings with incredible speed in full view of the customers adds to their deliciousness. Big parties of diners go there just for the dumplings and with this really simple sauce they are absolutely addictive. Fang is one of those places where you feel instantly euphoric. So simple are these one-pot wontons that I've had to add a little side order of mine, Asian slaw. I hope you love the combination as much as I do.

Mix together the slaw dressing ingredients.

To make the slaw, finely shred the cabbage and mix it with the other ingredients. Toss with the slaw dressing.

Steam the dumplings or microwave them according to the packet instructions.

Mix together the dipping sauce ingredients and serve alongside the steamed dumplings and slaw. You could also add some noodles with the same dressing – there will be enough to coat the noodles.

Quick cassoulet

SERVES 4

2 pieces of duck confit, from a tin or jar
100g smoked bacon lardons
150g smoked garlic sausage (I like Polish smoked sausage), thickly sliced on the diagonal
1 onion, finely sliced
4 garlic cloves, chopped
2 x 400g tins of haricot beans, drained
3 tomatoes, roughly chopped
300ml chicken stock
3–4 thyme sprigs, leaves stripped from the stalks
Handful of flatleaf parsley, roughly chopped
Salt and black pepper

To serve
Green salad

Some might say a quick cassoulet is sacrilege but, much as I love cassoulet, for the proper version you do need to settle down to a long afternoon of preparation involving nostalgic memories and several bottles of red wine, such as Madiran or Cahors, then a plethora of indigestion tablets in the middle of the night. You can prepare this recipe to the pre-oven stage the day before, if you like, then bring it up to temperature on the hob the next day and finish it in the oven for half an hour. If feeding a big crowd, simply double the quantities and use a larger casserole dish.

Preheat the oven to 170°C/Fan 150°C. Heat a couple of tablespoons of duck fat from the confit in a shallow ovenproof casserole dish. Fry the duck pieces until the skin is golden, then transfer them to a plate.

Add the bacon lardons and sausage to the fat in the casserole dish and fry until lightly browned. Add the onion and garlic and cook until golden, then add the beans, tomatoes, stock and thyme. Bring to the boil and simmer until the tomatoes have broken down.

Stir in the parsley and season to taste. Nestle the duck pieces among the beans, then put the casserole dish in the oven, uncovered. Leave the cassoulet to cook for about 30 minutes until piping hot and some of the liquid has evaporated. The duck will be very tender and easy to break up into servings. Good with a salad.

One-pot meatballs with tomato sauce & orzo

SERVES 4

400g premium pork sausages, skins removed and discarded
¾ tsp fennel seeds, coarsely ground
¼ tsp chilli flakes
4 tbsp olive oil
250g orzo
3 garlic cloves, chopped
60ml white wine
400ml soffritto passata (I like Napolina)
1 rosemary sprig
Salt and black pepper

To serve
Parmesan, grated
Basil leaves, torn

I tried making these meatballs with minced pork but they were too dry, so I think they are much better made with good-quality sausage meat, by which I mean at least 90 per cent pork. A lot of the brands of tomato passata with flavourings are not to my taste, but the Napolina soffritto is just tomato, garlic, onion and celery.

Mix the sausage meat, fennel seeds and chilli flakes in a bowl and shape the mixture into balls about the size of cherry tomatoes.

Heat 2 tablespoons of the olive oil in a shallow ovenproof casserole dish or a large pan with a lid and fry the meatballs until lightly browned all over. Transfer them to a plate and then set aside.

Add the remaining oil to the pan, add the orzo and fry for a couple of minutes. Add the garlic and fry for a minute, then pour in the wine and bring to the boil. Add the passata and 650ml of water, season and bring to the boil again. Turn the heat down to a simmer and cook for 2–3 minutes.

Add the meatballs and rosemary, season with salt and black pepper, then cover the pan with a lid and leave to simmer for about 10 minutes. Remove the lid and cook for a final couple of minutes until the orzo is done and the sauce is thickened.

Serve with plenty of freshly grated Parmesan cheese and torn basil leaves.

Caldo verde

SERVES 4
3 tbsp olive oil
1 onion, finely chopped
1 garlic clove, finely chopped
225g chorizo sausage, sliced
400g potatoes, preferably floury, peeled and cut into chunks
1.75 litres vegetable stock or water
300g spring greens or kale, shredded
Large pinch of chilli flakes, to serve
Salt and black pepper

Will our love for chorizo ever fade I wonder? In my memoir Under a Mackerel Sky *I wrote about Martin Leeburn, a friend at Oxford, who in the early seventies appeared at our student house with a couple of chorizos – he'd been to Spain for a year as a language student – and I will always remember that first hot smoky taste. Portuguese chorizo is just as good as Spanish and that's the secret of caldo verde. It's the combination of pork, smoky paprika and garlic with the potato thickening and brilliant green and slightly bitter kale that makes this such an unforgettable dish. Normally in Portugal the cabbage is very thinly sliced, using a special slicer, but I prefer to cut it a bit wider. And I have to own up to slightly jazzing things up with chilli flakes and extra chorizo.*

Warm the oil in a large pan and fry the onion, garlic and chorizo for 5–8 minutes until the onion is translucent. Add the potatoes and the stock or water and boil for about 10 minutes until the potatoes are cooked.

Pulverise the potatoes in the broth with a potato masher. Add the spring greens and bring back to the boil, then simmer for 4–5 minutes until the spring greens are cooked but still a vibrant green.

Season with salt and pepper, then serve, sprinkled with chilli flakes, in warm bowls.

Turkish spiced cabbage & minced lamb
Kapuska

SERVES 4
3 tbsp olive oil
250g minced lamb
2 onions, chopped
1 large garlic clove, chopped
1 tbsp tomato paste
1½ tbsp harissa paste
400g tin of chopped tomatoes
1 medium Savoy or white cabbage
Large pinch of chilli flakes
Salt and black pepper

I am never going to be vegetarian, but I do find more and more that I like eating lots of vegetables and very little meat. This is not a particularly new concept – after all, that's what beef with Yorkshire pudding and veg is all about – but now I will quite often serve no more than 80 grams of grilled steak per person with maybe a couple of little salads. It's the knowledge that there's some meat there, which satisfies me but what I am really loving is the rest of the meal. I'm almost using meat as a seasoning. So, kapuska is for me a perfect main course, as there's a small amount of minced lamb with tomato, plenty of cabbage and lots of spice.

Heat a tablespoon of the olive oil in a large pan over a high heat and fry the minced lamb until brown all over. Reduce the heat to medium, add the rest of the olive oil, the onions and garlic, and stir until the onions have softened.

Add the tomato paste, harissa and tomatoes, then season well with salt and pepper. Cook for a few minutes, add 375ml of water and bring to a simmer. Put a lid on the pan and leave to cook for 20 minutes.

Add the cabbage and simmer for about 30 minutes. Sprinkle with the chilli flakes and serve. Nice with crusty bread.

Sausages with lentils & cider

SERVES 4
1 tbsp oil
8 sausages
30g butter
1 red onion, chopped
2 garlic cloves, chopped
2 celery sticks, chopped
3 carrots, cut into small dice
2 tbsp plain flour
200ml cider
300ml chicken stock
2–3 thyme sprigs
250g ready-cooked puy lentils
Soy sauce
Handful of flatleaf parsley, roughly chopped
Dijon mustard, to serve
Salt and black pepper

This is the sort of dish that's nice to have a trayful of in the kitchen, keeping warm, so everybody can help themselves when they come in on a cold evening after Brownies, football practice, fireworks, swimming lessons or just a walk. Tonight is icy cold but crystal clear and I'm writing this as I sit, watching the fire, after a walk on Constantine beach. I'm reminded of a couple of lines from 'Frost at Midnight' by Samuel Taylor Coleridge:

'... Sea, and hill, and wood,
With all the numberless goings-on of life
Inaudible as dreams! The thin blue flame
Lies on my low-burnt fire and quivers not;'

Heat the oil in a shallow, flameproof casserole dish. Add the sausages and brown them all over, then continue to cook for another 5 minutes. Remove them from the pan and set aside on a plate.

Melt the butter in the pan, add the chopped onion, garlic, celery and carrots and fry gently for 5 minutes or so until softened and golden brown. Add the flour and cook for a minute, then pour in the cider and stock and add the thyme. Bring to the boil to thicken for a minute or so.

Cut each sausage into 3 on the diagonal and add them to the vegetables. Stir in the lentils, then turn the heat down to a simmer, cover the pan and cook for a few more minutes until the sausages are done. Season with salt and pepper and a few splashes of soy sauce, then stir in the parsley.

Serve with Dijon mustard and perhaps some green beans.

Beef stifado

SERVES 6
4 tbsp olive oil
1.2kg stewing/chuck steak, cut into chunks
600g round shallots, peeled but left whole
7 garlic cloves, sliced
1 tsp sugar
7cm piece of cinnamon stick
7 cloves
1 star anise
3 tbsp red wine vinegar
900ml red wine
1½ tins (600g) of chopped tomatoes
Salt and black pepper

To serve
Orzo, rice or sautéed potatoes

The idea, but not the actual recipe, for this comes from a rather lovely restaurant in Lindos called Kalypso on the island of Rhodes. I particularly like this dish because it's flavoured with star anise as well as cinnamon and cloves, and when I ate it at the restaurant I just couldn't work out what was so special about it. I had to ask Evripides Gkogkos, the chef/owner, what it was. Star anise is not a spice used much in Greece but I do like dishes that have an unexpected flavour that really works. I love stifado – the beef is always tender, delicious and falling apart and there's a nice simplicity about the sauce and the round shallots.

Preheat the oven to 180°C/Fan 160°C. Heat the olive oil in a large flameproof casserole dish and brown the meat all over in batches. Transfer each batch to a plate.

Add the shallots and garlic and gently fry them with the sugar until golden. Add the spices, then the vinegar, red wine and tomatoes and bring to the boil. Turn the heat down to a simmer right away, put the beef back in the casserole dish and season with salt and pepper.

Cover the dish with a lid, put it in the oven and leave to cook for about an hour. Check to see if the liquid looks very thick and add a little water, if necessary. Cover again and cook for a further 45–60 minutes or until the meat is tender and starting to fall apart. Serve with orzo or with rice or sautéed potatoes (see page 296).

VEGGIE SUPPERS

I don't really like to think of a dish as being vegetarian or not. It's just not the way I cook. Most of the time when I'm cooking for myself I like to include a little meat or fish, almost as a seasoning, but it's the vegetables I'm really interested in. I love vegetables. For example, at home I'll quite often grill a small amount of steak, just 70 or 80 grams, to go with a great mound of buttered hispi cabbage, which is around at about the same time that the season's first new potatoes are coming in from Spain and there's plenty of spearmint in the garden. Somehow the steak just sets the vegetables off; maybe it's partly to do with the contrast in texture. In the same way, I always add a pinch of salt to sweet dishes.

I suppose it's not just about meat, it's about umami – rather an overused word these days – which is often supplied by cheese, dried mushrooms, soy sauce or things like caramelised onions or slow-cooked aubergines. Personally, I don't subscribe to the idea that we should never eat animals or dairy produce for moral reasons. I do, however, think it's important to challenge the overconsumption of protein. We still do eat too much meat and actually, as it happens, not enough fish which is, I believe, due to the presence of omega-3 in virtually all seafood, vital to the healthy function of the brain.

Soon after I write this, I am off to India, and what I'm looking forward to most, apart from another visit to the Taj Mahal – which always lives up to one's memory of how incredibly special it is – is the food. In particular I'm anticipating having plenty of good vegetarian food. In India, though, there's never a feeling of being vegetarian or non-vegetarian because nearly half the population is vegetarian.

I think the recipes in this chapter are a sort of testimony to the way our cuisine is changing from meals that we used to refer to as meat and two veg to something much more inclusive of the cuisines of the world. Nowadays, we don't want to eat so much meat, we want to eat cheaply and healthily and we love exciting new flavours.

Take the whole roasted and spiced cauliflower (page 139) for example. When I was growing up, cauliflower was just an accompaniment to a roast and the most daring thing one did with it, lovely as it was, was to put it in béchamel sauce with cheese. But no more than twenty years ago, people started roasting the whole thing – sometimes parboiling it first, sometimes just putting it in the oven raw – and suddenly a rather boring vegetable became a wonderful main course.

Pasta also lends itself well to meals without meat. For a boy who grew up eating spaghetti with tomato sauce from a tin, the spaghetti with slow-cooked courgettes, rosemary and mascarpone (page 130) is a delight.

One thing to mention. If you are a strict vegetarian, rather than someone who wants to eat more veg and less meat, you might want to substitute vegetarian cheeses in some of the following recipes.

Gruyère & asparagus quiche

SERVES 4

15g butter
2 spring onions, sliced on the diagonal
8 asparagus spears, each cut into 3
125ml double cream
3 eggs, beaten
70g Gruyère cheese, grated
1 x 20–22cm baked savoury pastry case
Salt and black pepper

Making a quiche is so simple. The time-consuming bit is making the pastry case, but I have found that bought pastry cases are as good as home-made and if anything, they stay crisper for longer. Do make sure that you only bake the quiche until, as I say, it is just set because then the centre will be gorgeously soft and silky. If you would prefer to make your own pastry, you'll find a recipe on page 302.

Preheat the oven to 160°C/Fan 140°C.

Melt the butter in a frying pan, add the spring onions and asparagus (reserve 5 or 6 tips for later) and fry for a couple of minutes.

Mix the spring onions and asparagus (except the reserved pieces) with the cream, beaten eggs and cheese in a bowl. Season with salt and pepper and pour the mixture into the pastry case, then arrange the reserved asparagus on top. Bake for 20–25 minutes until just set.

Allow to cool for at least 10 minutes, before serving warm. A green salad and new potatoes are good accompaniments.

Mushroom & thyme tart

SERVES 4
320g pack of ready-rolled puff pastry

Topping
250g crème fraiche
150g fresh spinach, chopped or 125g frozen spinach
20g butter
1 onion, halved and finely sliced
1 garlic clove, finely chopped
200g mushrooms, sliced
4 or 5 thyme sprigs, stalks removed
150g Gruyère or Comté cheese, grated
Salt and black pepper

The idea for this came from the French version of pizza, tarte flambée, which we featured in my TV series Secret France. *It was such a crowd pleaser, I decided to make a vegetarian version, so I must confess all I have done here is substituted the bacon lardons in the original recipe with mushrooms and spinach. The only other change I have made is to use a puff pastry sheet from the supermarket instead of a dough base.*

Preheat the oven to 230°C/Fan 210°C. Lay the pastry sheet on a baking tray and prick it all over with a fork. Spread the crème fraiche over the pastry.

Wilt the spinach in a pan with just the water clinging to the leaves after washing, or, if using frozen spinach, warm it until defrosted. Drain well and squeeze out the excess liquid. Spread the spinach over the crème fraiche.

Melt the butter in a pan, add the onion and garlic and cook for a few minutes. Add the mushrooms and thyme and cook over a medium-high heat until golden. Spread the mixture on top of the spinach, sprinkle with the grated cheese and season with plenty of black pepper.

Bake in the oven for about 15–20 minutes until the base is crisp and the topping is golden and bubbling. Cut into squares and serve immediately, perhaps with a salad.

The bewildering way the young cook these days

My stepdaughter, Olive, and Flo, daughter of my assistant Portia, fill the fridge with jars of pesto, tomato and garlic soffritto, not just straight lardons but chorizo lardons, miso paste, tahini, Thai curry pastes, flavoured mayonnaises, piri piri mayo, Korean sauce, and so on. I've come to the conclusion that they are the custodians of simple suppers, simply because they have no snobbishness about buying whatever looks good and they both cook very tasty food. They don't really read recipe books; they pick ideas from TikTok, Instagram and YouTube.

Perhaps at my age I should be lamenting the end of the future generations doing 'proper cooking' from cookery books, but that would be wrong as the young do buy lots of books that they flick through for inspiration. Titles like *Leon Fast Vegetarian, The Roasting Tin, Mob Kitchen, Deliciously Ella* and *Jamie's 5 Ingredients*.

As far as I am concerned, I cook from recipe books. I don't just flick through them and I have them propped up in the kitchen if I'm not familiar with the dish. I like the feel of cookery books. I like turning the pages when I'm thinking about what to cook and I feel obliged to pencil notes in the margins if things aren't quite as I'd like them – notes like: double the garlic, add more chillies and salt.

I guess the reason I'm very interested in what Olive and Flo are doing in the kitchen is the same reason I'm still interested in music. I like the music Olive likes, although I am not sure what she feels about rap but it's not my cup of tea. We all went to Hawaii for my seventieth birthday with my sons as well and my fondest memory of the trip was driving along the north shore checking the surfing breaks, with my boys and step-kids playing their selection of music in open-top cars, a Ford Mustang and a Camaro.

My stepson Zach came up with the idea of starting a YouTube channel, initially just doing easy-to-cook fish dishes but subsequently featuring lots of my recipes from the past. Most of the recipes from this book will, in time, appear there. Actually, it wasn't just Zach's idea. During lockdown I started videoing myself cooking simple dishes without the benefit of the considerable enhancement of good cameras and skilled camera operators, sound recordists and directors. Looking back on some of these videos I wince a bit, but they did give me a chance to get into a different way of communicating, via YouTube and TikTok.

The other thing that has helped me understand the way that food and cooking moves on is that when I film somewhere like India or Istanbul, I like to get hold of a few bloggers who are making their own online videos. At university I studied language and I always remember the point that language is a living thing. I love the pompous way that the French try to exclude certain Anglo-Saxon words from their lexicon, and I think it's like King Canute trying to stop the waves.

I say: let cookery evolve and change. I think that the internet and the ability we have now to make our own little videos on cooking techniques has made cooking as easily approachable and understandable as language.

'I like the feel of cookery books. I like turning the pages when I'm thinking about what to cook and I feel obliged to pencil notes in the margins if things aren't quite as I'd like them.'

Baked aubergines with tomatoes, garlic & feta

SERVES 4

4 medium aubergines
150ml extra virgin olive oil
6 garlic cloves, finely chopped
2 x 400g tins of chopped tomatoes
2 tbsp tomato paste
2 tsp Greek oregano
200g feta cheese, cubed
Salt and black pepper

This dish is a mainstay of many a taverna in Greece. It's often served in a round terracotta dish, like a Spanish cazuela, but occasionally the aubergines come simply baked in their skins, then smothered in a tomato, garlic and oregano sauce and sprinkled with feta which I think looks really nice. If you want to make this a more substantial meal, serve it with rice or orzo pasta.

Preheat the oven to 200°C/Fan 180°C.

Halve the aubergines lengthways and score the insides in a diamond pattern. Place them cut-side up in a ceramic lasagne-type dish. Liberally brush the aubergines with olive oil and season well with salt and pepper.

Bake for about 30 minutes until really tender. Then turn the oven down to 160°C/Fan 140°C.

While the aubergines are cooking, heat the rest of the olive oil in a pan over a low heat and add the garlic. Cook gently for a minute, then add the tomatoes and tomato paste and season with salt, pepper and oregano. Continue to simmer over a low heat for about 25 minutes.

Pour the sauce over the baked aubergines and put the dish back in the oven for another 20 minutes or so. Sprinkle with feta and serve with crusty bread.

Roasted butternut squash with za'atar & chickpea salad

SERVES 4
1 butternut squash (about 1.2kg)
3 tbsp olive oil
1 tbsp za'atar
Salt and black pepper

Chickpea salad
200g cherry tomatoes, halved
½ cucumber, diced
1 small red onion, finely sliced
400g tin of chickpeas, drained
1 garlic clove, finely chopped or grated
Handful of fresh coriander, chopped, plus extra to garnish
¼ tsp chilli flakes

Dressing
2 tbsp tahini
Juice of ½ lemon
1 tbsp olive oil
Salt

To serve
Flatbreads (or see my recipe for Greek flatbreads p.301)
Extra virgin olive oil
Za'atar

It seems that whenever you go for supper with friends these days a butternut squash salad will appear. I must confess to have had a bit of a downer on butternut squash in the past, largely because these salads are often rather bland. Rather arrogantly, I determined to come up with a version that would be anything but. I'll leave you to make up your own mind as to whether I have succeeded.

Preheat the oven to 200°C/Fan 180°C. Peel the butternut squash, remove the seeds and dice the flesh into cubes.

Toss the butternut squash cubes with the olive oil and za'atar, then season with salt and pepper. Tip the squash into a baking tin and roast for 25–30 minutes, then remove and leave to cool to room temperature.

Put the squash in a serving dish, mix the salad ingredients together and serve on top of the squash. Mix the dressing ingredients together and dress the salad, then garnish with a little more chopped coriander.

Toast the flatbreads, brush them with olive oil and sprinkle with za'atar, then serve with the squash and salad.

Roasted nectarine salad with feta & mint

SERVES 4 AS A SIDE OR 2 AS A LIGHT SUPPER

3 tbsp olive oil
2 tbsp runny honey
6 nectarines, stoned and halved
2 red onions, cut into wedges
80g pea shoots or lamb's lettuce
150g feta, crumbled
A few mint sprigs, leaves only, roughly torn
30g almonds, roughly chopped

Vinaigrette

1 tbsp red wine vinegar
2 tsp runny honey
3 tbsp olive oil
Salt and black pepper

Salty cheese, fruit and mint with a bit of honey in there too is the sort of salad that makes me long to be back in Sydney. I remember a lunch at the house of a famous, now sadly departed, art dealer named Ray Hughes, and a long table surrounded by great works of art including a couple by one of the guests, Tim Storrier. The table was literally one long line of large platters of salads like this one, with acres of prosciutto, melon, halloumi, pomegranates, prawns, oysters and lots of basil everywhere, all partnered with sensational Chardonnays. It was one of those lunches you never want to end.

Preheat the oven to 200°C/Fan 180°C. Mix the olive oil and honey together in a roasting tin, add the nectarines and red onions, then toss to coat. Roast in the oven for about 20 minutes until tender, then leave to cool to room temperature.

Mix the vinaigrette ingredients together in a jug and season with salt and pepper.

Scatter the pea shoots or lamb's lettuce over a serving dish and arrange the nectarines and red onions on top. Pour over any roasting juices. Add the feta, scatter over the mint and almonds, then dress with the vinaigrette at the table. *Recipe photographs overleaf.*

Black bean burgers with Mexican slaw

SERVES 4
Vegetable oil
1 onion, finely chopped
2 garlic cloves, finely chopped
1 large red or green chilli, finely chopped
2 tsp ground cumin
2 x 400g tins of black beans, drained
120g mature Cheddar (such as Davidstow 36-month), crumbled
3–4 tbsp plain flour, plus extra for dusting
4 brioche buns
1 tomato, thinly sliced
Salt and black pepper

Slaw
About 180g white cabbage, shredded
1 small red onion, finely sliced
Large handful of fresh coriander, chopped
1 small green chilli, finely chopped
Juice of 1 lime

Chipotle crema
2 tsp chipotle paste
2 tbsp mayonnaise
2 tbsp soured cream

TIP
After I toast my burger buns, I burn them a little on the gas flame to give them a nice barbecue flavour.

I keep being offered burgers that look and try to taste like beef. I think if you use something completely different but make it up as a burger with some other great ingredients, particularly chipotle crema, you create something just as good but far cheaper.

Mix together all the slaw ingredients and set aside. Mix together the chipotle crema ingredients and set aside.

Heat 2 tablespoons of oil in a pan and fry the onion, garlic, chilli and cumin over a medium heat. When the onion has softened, add the black beans and cook for 5 minutes. Use a potato masher to partially break up the beans (this helps the burgers stick together) and season with salt and pepper. Add the cheese and bind the mixture together with the flour.

Form the mixture into 4 patties and dust with more flour. Heat some oil in a frying pan over a medium heat, add the bean burgers and fry them for 2–3 minutes on each side.

Toast the buns and serve the burgers in the buns, topped with sliced tomato, coleslaw and chipotle crema.

Spaghetti with courgettes, rosemary & mascarpone

SERVES 4

4 tbsp olive oil
600g courgettes, grated
1 garlic clove, chopped
Zest of ½ unwaxed lemon
1 tsp chopped fresh rosemary leaves
¼ tsp chilli flakes
90g mascarpone
50g Pecorino or Parmesan cheese, grated
400g spaghetti
Salt and black pepper

This is one of those Italian pasta recipes that's so simple you can't believe how wonderful it tastes when you check the ingredients. I can't think of any basic food where the expression 'less is more' fits better than with pasta. It's a source of some irritation to me that some people in the UK still think that the ratio of sauce to pasta should be at least 50/50 if not 70/30. Am I alone in finding a mound of tomato sauce with a few strings of spaghetti a profoundly depressing sight?

Heat the olive oil in a large pan and add the grated courgettes, garlic, lemon zest, rosemary and chilli flakes. Cook gently over a medium-low heat for 20–25 minutes until the courgettes are very soft. Stir in the mascarpone and two-thirds of the cheese, then taste and season with salt and plenty of pepper.

Cook the spaghetti in salted boiling water according to the packet instructions. Drain, add the pasta to the courgette sauce and stir well to combine. Serve topped with the remaining grated cheese and freshly ground black pepper.

Yellow dal with spinach & roasted vegetables

SERVES 4

Dal
250g chana dal, soaked for an hour in cold water, then drained
2 tomatoes, chopped
1 onion, chopped
2 garlic cloves, peeled and bashed
4 green chillies, slit lengthways
5 or 6 curry leaves
1 tsp salt
½ tsp turmeric
250g spinach leaves, washed, or 175g frozen spinach, defrosted

Roasted vegetables
1 aubergine, cut into large cubes
1 red onion, peeled and cut into 8 wedges
4 carrots, peeled and cut into chunks on the diagonal
3 tbsp vegetable oil
2 tsp garam masala
Salt and black pepper

To finish
2 tsp vegetable oil
1 tsp black mustard seeds
1 red chilli, chopped

To serve
Handful of coriander, chopped

I've made the basis of this a tarka dal. This is a yellow dal finished with a tarka, which is quickly fried black mustard seeds and chilli. I also stir in some spinach and top the dish with roasted, spiced aubergine, red onion and carrots.

Put the soaked dal in a saucepan and cover with about 4cm of cold water. Add the remaining dal ingredients, except the spinach, and bring to the boil, then simmer for 1–1½ hours until the dal is tender. Using a potato masher, mash the dal roughly so that it still has some texture. Add the spinach and stir it through until wilted.

While the dal is cooking, preheat the oven to 200°C/Fan 180°C. Put all the vegetables in a roasting tin and toss them with the oil and garam masala, then season with salt and pepper. Roast for about 25 minutes or until tender.

To finish, heat the 2 teaspoons of oil in a small pan. When it's hot, add the mustard seeds and when they are popping, add the chilli. Take the pan off the heat.

Divide the dal between 4 bowls, top with roasted vegetables and the mustard seed oil, then sprinkle with coriander.

A deep red wine vegetable stew with thyme dumplings

SERVES 6
15g dried porcini mushrooms
150ml of just-boiled water
2 tbsp oil
1 large onion, sliced
2 garlic cloves, chopped
1 tbsp tomato paste
1 tsp brown sugar
4 large carrots, cut into chunks
1 celeriac (about 850g) peeled, trimmed and cut into chunks
6 waxy potatoes, scrubbed and halved
500ml red wine
500ml vegetable stock
1 rosemary sprig
400g tin of borlotti beans, drained
200g chestnut mushrooms, quartered
Handful of parsley, roughly chopped, to serve
Salt and black pepper

Dumplings
200g self-raising flour, plus extra for dusting
100g vegetable suet
Leaves from 1 thyme sprig, chopped
1 tsp salt
Black pepper

I tried to come up with a vegetarian version of boeuf bourguignon, but all I ended up saying to myself after a couple of experiments was, where's the beef? So I decided to use an old trick of mine for giving sauces for fish a bit of beefiness and used dried porcini in the stock and also more wine. Everybody who's tried this loves it, but really the secret of the dish is just that there's something so satisfying about dumplings.

Put the dried porcini mushrooms in a bowl and cover them with the just-boiled water. Leave to soak while you prepare the vegetables.

Preheat the oven to 180°C/Fan 160°C. Heat the oil in a flameproof casserole dish, add the onion and garlic and cook over a medium heat until softened. Add the tomato paste, sugar, carrots, celeriac and potatoes. Pour over the red wine, vegetable stock and the porcini mushrooms and their liquid, but hold back on the last tablespoon of the mushroom liquid as it might be gritty.

Bring to the boil, season with salt and pepper and add the sprig of rosemary. Put a lid on the casserole dish, place it in the oven and cook for about 50 minutes.

When the dish has been cooking for about 45 minutes, mix together all the ingredients for the dumplings in a large bowl. Add enough cold water – about 150ml – to bind the mixture to a soft dough.

Take the dish out of the oven and stir in the borlotti beans and chestnut mushrooms. Check the seasoning. With floured hands, roll the dumpling dough into 6 balls and arrange them on top of the vegetables. Put the dish back in the oven, uncovered, for about 20 minutes until the dumplings are well risen and lightly golden. Sprinkle over the parsley and serve. Good with steamed greens and mustard.

Goat's cheese & thyme soufflés

SERVES 6

Oil, for greasing
85g unsalted butter
85g plain flour
1 tsp dry mustard powder
550ml whole milk
30g Pecorino cheese, grated
2 tsp chopped thyme leaves
4 large eggs, separated
175g goat's cheese, crumbled
Salt and black pepper

There's nothing difficult about soufflés, but my earnest advice is to get them made, spooned into the ramekins and in the fridge earlier in the day, rather than leaving it all to the last minute. Just remember to get them out twenty minutes before baking, so they can come up to room temperature. And, as with Yorkshire puddings, once the soufflés are in the oven, don't open the door. The drop in temperature may well cause the air trapped inside the mixture to contract and collapse the soufflés.

Grease 6 ramekins well with oil. Melt the 85g of butter in a large saucepan, add the flour and mustard powder and mix well. Cook for a few minutes, stirring constantly, then gradually whisk in the milk, a little at a time, until you have a thick, smooth mixture. Stir in the Pecorino and thyme, then set aside to cool slightly. Beat in the egg yolks and stir in the crumbled goat's cheese, then season with salt and pepper.

Whisk the egg whites in a clean bowl until they start to stiffen and hold peaks. Beat a spoonful of the whites into the cheesy mixture to loosen it. Then, using a large metal spoon, fold in the rest of the egg whites carefully, retaining as much air and lightness as possible.

Preheat the oven to 200°C/Fan 180°C. Spoon the mixture into the ramekins and bake for 12–15 minutes. Serve at once.

Halki pasta

SERVES 8
250g salted butter
1kg onions, chopped
1kg casarecce pasta
(or other short pasta
such as fusilli or penne)
150g Gruyère cheese,
grated
Olive oil
Salt and black pepper

I came across this on the island of Halki, near Rhodes. It didn't look like much but it tasted good. I think it's the slow cooking of the onions in masses of butter and the large amount of Graviera cheese (the Greek version of Gruyère) that makes it work so well. In a bar in Lindos last autumn, I got talking to the manager whose aunt, Zoe Kornarou, happened to be making this pasta dish for several of the local restaurants in Halki. He said they just couldn't get enough of it.

Melt the butter in a large pan, add the onions and cook them for about 30 minutes over a low heat until soft and golden. Season with a teaspoon of salt and some black pepper.

Boil the pasta in plenty of salted water until al dente and then drain well.

Grease a shallow oven dish with olive oil, add half the pasta and top with half the grated cheese. Then add the rest of the pasta and cheese, pour the onions over the top and let the mixture percolate through the pasta for a minute or so.

Season with salt and pepper and serve with a green salad.

Whole roasted & spiced cauliflower with pilau rice

SERVES 4
1 cauliflower (about 1kg)
4 tbsp groundnut or vegetable oil
3 tsp garam masala
½ tsp hot chilli powder
½ tsp turmeric
Fresh coriander leaves
Salt

Pilau rice
1 tsp vegetable oil
2 cloves
3cm piece of cinnamon stick
1 green cardamom pod, crushed
300g basmati rice

To serve
Mango chutney (shop-bought or see p.294)
Raita (shop-bought or see p.293)

I have tried to keep the ingredients here to the absolute minimum needed for good flavour, so the spicing is just garam masala, chilli and turmeric. This dish is absurdly easy but looks fantastic when it comes out of the oven. A thick slice of the cauliflower with some pilau rice is really special, but it does need something a bit wet to go with it; I suggest raita and mango chutney. I also like coriander chutney and you'll find a recipe for this on page 293.

Preheat the oven to 180°C/Fan 160°C. Trim all but the pale green leaves from the cauliflower and place it, whole, in a roasting tin of a similar size.

Mix the oil and spices with a teaspoon of salt, pour the mixture over the cauliflower, then rub it into the surface. Cover the whole tin with foil and roast the cauliflower in the oven for about 1–1¼ hours until tender. Remove the foil and baste the cauliflower with the oil in the tin – if it's dried out, add a teaspoon of water. Cook the cauliflower for another 10 minutes without the foil.

Meanwhile, cook the rice. Heat the oil in a saucepan and fry the spices for 30 seconds until they smell aromatic. Add the rice to the pan with a quarter of a teaspoon of salt, then stir briefly. Add 400ml of water and bring it to the boil. Put a lid on the pan and cook the rice over a very low heat for 10–12 minutes until all the water has been absorbed.

Serve the rice with the cauliflower cut into wedges and mango chutney and raita on the side. *Recipe photographs overleaf.*

Radicchio & red onion tart

SERVES 4

25g butter
1 small red onion, finely sliced
1 tsp sugar
140g radicchio or red/white chicory
3 medium eggs
150ml double cream
Leaves from a thyme sprig
1 tsp Dijon mustard
1 x 22cm savoury pastry case
60g Gruyère or mature Cheddar or vintage Gouda
Salt and black pepper

TIP

If you prefer to make your own pastry, there's a recipe on page 302. And if you are using a 23cm tart tin you will need to increase the filling a little. I suggest using 250g of radicchio and 200ml of cream – the rest of the ingredients should be fine.

I came up with the idea for a radicchio and red onion tart after a trip I made to Soul Farm, near Falmouth, on my third series of Rick Stein's Cornwall. *The radicchio was superb and I wanted to cook with it as the Italians often do, but we seldom think of in the UK. It's often just relegated to salads but the marriage in this tart of cooked, slightly bitter radicchio with caramelised red onion is delicious. If you can't get radicchio, you can substitute red or white chicory.*

Preheat the oven to 160°C/Fan 140°C. Melt the butter in a large frying pan. Add the onion and sugar and cook over a low-medium heat for about 5 minutes until soft. Add the sliced radicchio or chicory and cook for 4–5 minutes until soft and wilted.

Whisk the eggs in a bowl, then add the cream and thyme and season with salt and pepper. Smooth the mustard over the base of the pastry case and arrange the onion and radicchio on top. Scatter over half the cheese, then pour in the cream mixture. Sprinkle the remaining cheese on top and bake for about 25 minutes until softly set.

Leave to cool in the tin for 15 minutes or so, then cut into wedges and serve with a green salad.

Panzanella

SERVES 4

1 good-sized sourdough or ciabatta loaf (about 300g)
½ cucumber
750g good tomatoes, preferably a mix of types and sizes
2 garlic cloves, crushed or grated
2 tbsp red wine vinegar
4 tbsp extra virgin olive oil, plus extra to serve
1 roasted red pepper, from a jar, drained and cut into strips
1 small red onion, very thinly sliced
2 tbsp capers in brine, drained and rinsed
100g small, well flavoured black olives
Handful of basil leaves, torn into pieces
Salt and black pepper

I have noticed that recipes like this are common in all Mediterranean countries, particularly Spain and Greece. I've quite often had a Greek salad that included rusk-like bread, for example. It just adds another dimension of texture and flavour to a salad. You do need the best tomatoes for this, and now you can make it at any time of year, even in winter, thanks to the availability of top-of-the-range cherry tomatoes.

Lightly toast the bread and break it into pieces. Peel the cucumber, cut it in half lengthways and scoop out the seeds with a teaspoon. Cut the 2 halves across into slices and set them aside.

Roughly chop the tomatoes and put them in a salad bowl with all the juices and seeds. Add the garlic and stir in the vinegar, olive oil and some seasoning.

Five minutes before serving, add the pieces of bread to the salad bowl and toss well with the tomatoes. Add the cucumber, red pepper, red onion, capers, olives and basil and check the seasoning. Set aside for 5 minutes to allow time for the bread to soften slightly.

Serve, drizzled with a little more extra virgin olive oil and sprinkled with sea salt and freshly ground black pepper.

SUPPERS FOR ONE

I wonder if there's a general truth in my belief that the world splits into those who like to cook for themselves and those who regard it as depressing and would sooner get a takeaway. You probably don't need great perspicacity to see that I'm very much in the first camp, but my wife, Sas, would never dream of cooking for herself. Maybe it's more a split of introverts and extroverts. I suppose I'm lucky because a lot of the time when I'm cooking for myself I'm also working on recipe ideas. Nevertheless, the thought of picking up a wild sea bass at our fish shop in Padstow fills me with such excited anticipation that I create a whole fantasy world of what to cook with it and, almost more importantly, what to drink with it.

I get a bit embarrassed by my TV programmes, especially when Sas says, 'You're on again' and I always seem to be in a market somewhere, banging on about red mullet, squid or razor clams, or picking up a stiff, fresh bass with green seaweed still partly covering its skin and spines and with a smell of the sea. The older I get, the more I realise that the prospect of cooking something memorable using some fabulous ingredient excites me more than anything else in life. When I made this slightly pompous announcement, David Pritchard, the director I worked with for twenty years, said, 'What about sex?' 'Absolutely, that includes sex', I replied, but a couple of moments later I added, 'Well maybe not sex, but everything else'. I firmly believe that the true wonder of something really good and simple is best experienced on your own. However, sharing a meal with one other person, or maybe even three or four who get what's so special about it, is the best way I know of deciding who your best friends really are.

In this chapter I've included just nine recipes that I've recently cooked for myself with my reasons as to what makes them so special. For me, the perfect simple supper is a whole lemon sole (page 165), all to myself. Of course, you can cook lemon sole for two, but I would suggest no more than two. Lemon sole is not quite as easy as Dover sole, as it has a softer flesh and you can't skin it so you have to make the skin an enjoyable part of the dish. If cooked properly, the skin should be a little crisp. When I get my lemon sole right, I reach for a bottle of white burgundy to accompany this beautiful dish.

The other thing about cooking just for yourself is the joy of making things up as you go along. For the first time last summer, I grew a little pot of tiny bush tomatoes and next to it three large oval pots of herbs. I planted a pot of basil from the supermarket and thanks to the extraordinarily hot, dry weather it flourished in London as well as it does in Sydney. I tried a tomato with a single basil leaf; the tomato was sweet and acidic, and I realised that basil, which the Greeks only grow to deter mosquitoes, is a herb that promises endless pleasure by its scent, but its flavour is only delivered in very rare combinations. One is with tomatoes and the other is in a cream-based white wine sauce for fish. Deep-fried basil tastes of nothing and added to any stew or hot vegetable it disappears, but with tomato and prosciutto it comes alive.

Armed with this thought I took a piece of honeydew melon from the fridge and wrapped Parma ham around it. I added four tiny quartered tomatoes and a lick of olive oil – extra virgin that a friend had given me in Greece. I got a chunk of old Parmesan and tried to shave it, but it ended up as big crumbles so I just added it to the plate, and I swear that was the best way of bringing out the flavour of basil I could ever have come up with. An afterthought: another special use of basil is in pesto, but I would never do that for a solo supper.

Egg Florentine

SERVES 1
150g fresh spinach
Small knob of butter
1 egg
40g mascarpone
15g Parmesan, grated
Few rasps of freshly grated nutmeg
Salt and black pepper

To serve
Sourdough bread

This is a simple version of the much-loved dish, using mascarpone and Parmesan rather than hollandaise. Actually, I sometimes find the combination in the classic recipe almost too rich, so in addition to being very quick and easy to make, this is also slightly more satisfying.

Wilt the spinach in a pan, add the butter and season with salt and pepper.

Bring a pan of water to a simmer and poach the egg.

In a separate pan, heat the mascarpone with 2 tablespoons of hot water to thin it a little, then add the grated Parmesan. Stir over a low heat until you have a smooth sauce.

Toast and butter the sourdough, add the wilted spinach, then top with a poached egg. Spoon over the cheese sauce and season with salt, pepper and a few rasps of nutmeg.

Easy croque monsieur

SERVES 1

2 tbsp full-fat crème fraiche
50g Gruyère or Comté cheese, grated
Few rasps of freshly grated nutmeg
Knob of soft butter
2 slices of bread
1 tsp Dijon mustard
1 thick slice of ham
Salt and black pepper

To serve
Green salad

The thing that puts most people off making croque monsieur is the béchamel sauce. Here, I'm just using crème fraiche and it's absolutely delicious.

Preheat the oven to 220°C/Fan 200°C.

Mix the crème fraiche with the grated cheese, then season with the nutmeg and salt and pepper. Butter each slice of bread on one side and place them on a baking tray, buttered-side up. Toast the buttered sides under a hot grill.

When the toast is golden, spread the untoasted side of one slice with mustard and top with the ham and half of the crème fraiche mixture. Top with the other piece of toast, buttered-side up, and spread over the remaining crème fraiche. Season with plenty of black pepper.

Put the baking tray in the oven and bake the croque monsieur for 10–12 minutes until it's golden and bubbling. Enjoy it with a green salad.

Late-night food

I've been thinking about the sorts of things I like to eat late in the evening, when supper is a distant memory, and I have to confess that the main reason for such hastily assembled dishes would be that I was pissed. I didn't think that a chapter titled alcohol-inspired suppers would look too good, but the reality is that the raging munchies that come upon you after an evening at the pub – which for us might well end with my wife dancing, not necessarily on the floor but sometimes on the table or on one occasion, on the bar top – requires a particular type of instant sustenance when you finally get back home.

Many people just eat all the chocolate in the fridge, but I have a curious love of a cereal that's reasonably rare in this country. It's called Grape-Nuts and I like it with lots of milk and at least two tablespoons of dark brown muscovado sugar. I collapse on the red sofa that's in front of our TV – a sofa that's so deep and comfortable it's hard to get up from – and can consume four bowls of cereal while watching whatever happens to come on. It might be a classic film, like *Whatever Happened to Baby Jane*, a programme about disused prisons in jungles or on Roman baths, or an ancient episode of *Grand Designs* or *QI*. Not one scintilla of any of this do I ever remember the next day.

Sometimes a late-night snack can be put together from your store cupboard or from what you normally keep in your fridge. And remember that this was how the famous Caesar salad came about: it was just an impromptu collection of ingredients that happened to be in the restaurant fridge somewhere in Tijuana. It would be nice to stop for a kebab at 12.30am in Padstow but that's not going to happen, so as I'm walking up the hill from The Golden Lion or The Old Ship, I often think about what I am going to devour when I get home. Cheese is high on the list, and I might just manage to knock up my simple version of croque monsieur (page 152), made without béchamel sauce but still nicely flavoured with nutmeg. Another thing I really love is a cheese omelette. Any cheese will do, even some thin slices of Camembert or some Saint Agur, a very ordinary blue cheese which I am addicted to and is available everywhere, not only in Padstow or London but also in Sydney. Other awful things are oven chips with a fried egg or a full English breakfast, preferably with sausages and baked beans. If there's any crab in the fridge it'll be gone in an instant, and in my last book I wrote about keeping a cold chicken in the fridge for snacks – that would be gone too.

My saving grace is that I don't like drinking alcohol just before going to bed. I love a pint of fizzy water with plenty of elderflower cordial. My wife, being Australian, always tries to make me have a Berocca but it's far too late for that sort of thing. I'll always promise to have it in the morning.

In this book you will find some other last-minute gems, including two dishes that I love at any time of day or night. The first, something that always hits the spot for me, is a pizza but made with a sheet of ready-made puff pastry or three sheets of filo, each one brushed with olive oil, instead of dough. You just need a basic tomato sauce – tomatoes and onions or tomatoes and garlic or tomatoes and peppers – things I always have in the fridge, then you can throw on whatever is available. My recipe for a quick pizza (page 19) has black olives, cheese and artichokes from a jar, but use whatever you like to have on a pizza or have available. The second dish is scrambled eggs (page 156), always a favourite.

'Something that always hits the spot for me, is a pizza but made with a sheet of ready-made puff pastry or three sheets of filo, each one brushed with olive oil, instead of dough.'

My ultimate scrambled eggs

SERVES 1
25g butter
2 eggs
1–2 tsp double cream
Salt and black pepper

To serve
Toast

Years ago I conducted an interview for chefs at L'Hotel in Knightsbridge, now called The Basil Street Hotel. My interview technique was a tad unusual: I just asked, 'How do you make scrambled eggs?' One young woman, Fiona Cock, replied, 'I don't know how you do it, but this is how I like them.' This showed me confidence and personal taste and she got the job and went on to be an excellent pastry chef. I don't know how you like your scrambled eggs, but this is how I like them. The secret is plenty of butter.

Melt the butter in a small frying pan over a low-medium heat. Beat the eggs with a fork and season with plenty of freshly ground black pepper and some salt.

Pour the eggs over the melted butter and leave them for 20 seconds before stirring. You want the eggs to start setting so you get nice chunks (I call them curds) of egg, then stir in the cream. The texture should be 'baveuse', slightly runny and soft set. Scoop out on to toast and eat immediately.

Noodles with stir-fried greens

SERVES 1

1 x 50g nest of dried egg noodles
Vegetable oil, for frying
10g root ginger, peeled and grated or finely chopped
1 garlic clove, finely chopped
½ red chilli, chopped, or a good pinch of chilli flakes
1 pak choi or about 150g spinach leaves
2 tsp soy sauce
1 egg
Sriracha chilli sauce, to serve
Salt

This is the sort of Southeast Asian dish I cook all the time at home for lunch or supper. The ingredients are not set in stone, but I guess the essentials are garlic, ginger, chilli and soy sauce. Some other thoughts for things to include might be tenderstem broccoli, mangetout, thinly sliced cabbage and coriander.

Cook the noodles in a pan of simmering, lightly salted water for 4–5 minutes, then drain well.

While the noodles are cooking, heat a tablespoon of oil in a frying pan or wok and add the ginger, garlic and chilli. Cook for 30 seconds, while stirring, then add the greens and keep them moving for a couple of minutes until they start to soften. Add 50ml of water and the soy sauce and cook for a minute or so until the greens have wilted.

Meanwhile, heat a little oil in a separate pan and fry the egg. Tip the noodles into a bowl, top with the greens and fried egg and serve with some chilli sauce.

Mushroom carbonara

SERVES 1
100g spaghetti
1 tbsp extra virgin olive oil
75g chestnut mushrooms, sliced
1 garlic clove, finely chopped
Small handful of flatleaf parsley, chopped
1 egg, beaten
20g Pecorino cheese, freshly grated
Salt and black pepper

I always feel a little bit hesitant about changing a main ingredient in a famous dish, in this case substituting mushrooms for pancetta or if you are being extremely purist, guanciale or cured pork jowl. However, apart from the meat, it's the Pecorino and the method of folding raw egg into hot pasta that's so special, and like this, it does make a fantastic vegetarian dish.

Bring a pan of water to the boil, add salt and cook the spaghetti until al dente.

Heat a large, deep frying pan over a medium-high heat, add the oil and mushrooms and fry until lightly golden. Add the garlic and parsley and cook for a few seconds, then remove the pan from the heat and set aside.

Drain the spaghetti well, then tip it into the frying pan with the mushrooms, garlic and parsley, Add the beaten egg and two-thirds of the grated cheese and toss together well.

Season to taste with a little salt and plenty of black pepper. The heat from the spaghetti will be sufficient to partly cook the egg but will still leave it moist and creamy. Serve in a warmed bowl, sprinkled with the rest of the grated cheese.

Tuna melt muffin with spring onion & capers

SERVES 1

- 80g tin of tuna, well drained
- 1 tbsp mayonnaise
- 1 spring onion, finely sliced
- 1 tsp capers, roughly chopped
- Pinch of chilli flakes
- 1 English muffin, cut in half
- 1 tomato, finely sliced
- 30g Cheddar or Gruyère, grated
- Black pepper

I have to say I am a latecomer to the world of melts, but now I wonder what took me so long. I guess I've always thought of them as not really a recipe, more like something in the words of a Dire Straits' song: 'that ain't cooking, that's the way you do it. Money for nothin'...' But this is lovely.

Mix together the tuna, mayonnaise, spring onion, capers and chilli flakes. Season with black pepper.

Toast the muffin, cut-side up, until lightly golden. Divide the tuna mix between the halves and top with sliced tomatoes and grated cheese.

Grill under a medium heat until the cheese is melted and bubbling. Serve with a salad.

Lemon sole meunière

SERVES 1
1 lemon sole (about 350g), skin on and head on, tight trimmed (see method)
Plain flour, for dusting
2 tbsp oil, for frying
25g butter
Juice of ¼ lemon
1 tbsp finely chopped parsley
1 tsp nonpareil capers
Salt and black pepper

A version of this is currently on the menu at our St Petroc's Bistro. It's called sole Joinville, which is the same dish but with a garnish of fried button mushrooms and brown shrimps. It's delicious, although a bridge slightly too far for a supper for one, but this simpler version I love too. It's really sensible to cut the sides of the fish off as I describe below; those little bones do get in the way.

To tight trim a lemon sole (or other flatfish), take a pair of sharp scissors and cut the frilly fins and the fleshy bones off both sides. You want to cut about 4cm off all round so that you are left with just the 4 fillets on the backbone.

Season both sides of the fish with salt and pepper and dust with plain flour.

Heat the oil in a frying pan over a medium heat. Add the sole, white-side down, and gently fry for 3–4 minutes. Turn the fish over and cook on the other side for a further 3 minutes. Transfer to a warm plate while you quickly make the sauce.

Add the butter to the pan and when it starts to foam, add the lemon juice, parsley and capers. Spoon the sauce down the length of the fish and serve immediately. I like to have some new potatoes and buttery hispi cabbage with my lemon sole.

Gnocchi with crab, chilli & parsley

SERVES 1
250g gnocchi
1 tbsp olive oil
1 garlic clove, chopped
Large pinch of chilli flakes
50g white crab meat
1 tbsp chopped flatleaf parsley
Squeeze of lemon juice
Salt and black pepper

I originally wrote this recipe to go on the menu at my restaurant Bannisters, in Mollymook, New South Wales, using langoustines from Western Australia and handmade gnocchi. This is a simpler version and very delicious.

Cook the gnocchi in salted water according to the packet instructions and drain well.

Heat the oil in a frying pan and gently fry the garlic. Turn off the heat and add the hot gnocchi, chilli flakes, crab meat, parsley and lemon juice. Season with salt and pepper and stir to coat the gnocchi well. Serve immediately.

Steak with chimichurri sauce & baked potato

SERVES 1
1 baking potato
Oil
200g hanger steak
Salt and black pepper

Chimichurri sauce
Small handful of flatleaf parsley, chopped
½ red chilli, deseeded and finely chopped
1 garlic clove, finely chopped or grated
2 tbsp olive oil
1½ tsp red wine vinegar
Good pinch of dried oregano

To serve
1 tbsp soured cream

A small frustration in my in my life is that I've never been to Argentina and so cannot be absolutely certain how chimichurri should taste. I feel a bit like those medieval artists who painted leopards, rhinos, crocodiles and elephants, although they had clearly never seen the real thing. But I'm inordinately fond of my own chimichurri and one day I'll take a little bottle of it to Buenos Aires.

Rub the potato in a little oil and season with plenty of salt and pepper. Bake at 200°C/Fan 180°C for an hour or until tender inside or cook it in a microwave if you prefer.

Take the steaks out of the fridge at least half an hour before cooking so they can come up to room temperature.

When the potato is ready, cook the steak. Heat a tablespoon of oil in a heavy frying pan and when it's hot add the steak and cook it to your liking, according to the timings below. Set the steak aside to rest for 5 minutes.

For the sauce, mix together the parsley, chilli, garlic, oil, vinegar and oregano and season with salt and pepper to taste. Once the steak has rested, slice it on the diagonal and dress it with the sauce. Serve with the jacket potato, soured cream and salad.

Cooking times for 2cm thick steak
I use a temperature probe placed in thickest part of the meat for checking steak. The temperatures below are just before taking the steak off the heat.

Blue: 1 minute on each side (47–49°C)
Rare: 1½ minutes on each side (50–52°C)
Medium rare: 2 minutes on each side (55°C)
Medium: 2¼ minutes on each side (60°C)
Medium well done: 2½–3 minutes on each side (65°C)
Well done: 4 minutes on each side (71°C)

SUPPERS FOR TWO

I used to write most of my recipes for four people. It seemed like a sensible number and often the maximum number of portions I felt you could cook in a normal kitchen, unless it was a roast or a pie. Four steaks, say, or four whole fish would be about as far as you could go. Latterly, however, I find some recipes are best cooked just for two. This is particularly true when last-minute timing is important or where there are a few bits and pieces, as in the bibimbap (page 204) where the ingredients are cooked individually one after another but all in the same pan. And a dish like chicken saltimbocca (page 190), where the final sauce is made in the pan in which the chicken is cooked is a bit of a hassle for more than two.

The other reason for cooking for two is when you want to make a fuss of somebody, such as your 'squeeze', as my wife would say, or just a good friend you want to have a serious chat with while also offering them something special to show how much you regard them.

I have to admit that this always makes me think of my mother. She used to do saltimboccas just for me and her and serve them with a soft green lettuce salad with a slightly sweetened vinegar and olive oil dressing; some chips would have been nice, but she never made a chip. But what she did do was lay the table in the kitchen near the blue Aga for the two of us with lace table napkins and she always bought a bottle of Alsace Gewürztraminer because she knew how much I liked it. It was Hugel's and one of my father's favourite wines.

I don't know what my mum would have made of the mackerel poke bowl (page 186), which although it is a cold dish does require some quite intricate last-minute preparation and presentation. For something like that, two servings are quite enough; more can make you a bit panicky. Poke is a lovely dish but unfortunately for me, I came to it rather late in life in Hawaii, where what I imagine had been a lovely local speciality had migrated to large trays in the supermarkets. Because it's so good, though, I still do make it but not with quite the same enthusiasm as that other raw fish dish, sashimi, which I was lucky enough to try for the first time in a little sushi restaurant just by the Tsukiji fish market in Tokyo.

All the dishes in this chapter are designed to be cooked without any lengthy preparation. Even the chickpea mash uses tinned ones that are mashed at the last minute.

Roasted tomatoes with burrata, anchovies & capers

SERVES 2

- 3 large tomatoes, halved
- 2 tbsp olive oil
- 1 x 150g burrata
- 4 anchovies, from a tin, each snipped into 3 or 4 pieces
- 1 tbsp capers, drained
- Handful of basil, leaves roughly torn
- Salt and black pepper

I can't believe there's anybody who doesn't love burrata. Apparently, it's been around since the fifties, though I've only known about it for the last five or ten years. Although it looks like a ball of mozzarella, burrata is actually mozzarella stuffed with stracciatella cheese and cream, which gives it such lusciousness and flavour that it almost makes mozzarella taste a bit boring by comparison. Like anything very creamy, it enhances the flavours you put with it. For me, that's always got to be olive oil, tomatoes and basil and why not some anchovies and capers for added saltiness and tartness.

Preheat the oven to 200°C/Fan 180°C. Arrange the tomato halves in a small roasting dish, drizzle them with olive oil and season with salt and pepper. Roast for 25–30 minutes until tender.

Put 3 tomato halves on each plate, then tear the burrata ball in half and add it to the tomatoes. Top with anchovies and capers and drizzle over the juices from the roasting pan. Scatter the basil on top, season with salt and pepper and serve with bread.

Halloumi, rocket & fig salad with strawberry dressing

SERVES 2 AS A MAIN COURSE OR MORE IF SERVING WITH OTHER DISHES

225g halloumi cheese, cut into 6 slices
Olive oil
120g bag of mixed rocket and spinach salad leaves
½ ripe avocado, sliced
6 soft dried figs, each cut into quarters

Dressing

150g ripe strawberries, puréed
2 tbsp olive oil
1 tbsp red wine vinegar
Salt and black pepper

When I remember what the cooking was like in Greece when I first started going there in the early seventies, it's almost hard to believe that I'm talking about the same country. My first memory of Greek cooking was a massive pan full of sheep heads in an orange stew in a restaurant just outside Igoumenitsa in northern Greece. I remember thinking at the time that I was going to starve. The reality, I now realise, was that Greek food then was not intended for tourists. These days the cooking in restaurants is generally fabulous and I have to say that much as I can see the negative effects of too much tourism, it doesn't half improve the food. Even dishes like moussaka, stifado and kleftiko are often really lovely, and I don't know whether baklava is made better than it used to be but I'm such an addict now. This interesting salad comes from an informal supper type of place called Plakostroto on the island of Hydra. I must say I have always been a bit wary of strawberry vinegar, thinking right back to the eighties when it was very much à la mode, but used as a vinaigrette here it's wonderful.

To make the dressing, mix the puréed strawberries, olive oil and vinegar and season with a pinch of salt and plenty of black pepper.

Brush the halloumi with a little oil and fry it over a high heat until brown on the underside. Turn it over and repeat on the second side.

Mix the salad leaves, avocado and figs together and top with the cooked halloumi slices. Drizzle over the strawberry dressing, then serve immediately.

Bubble & squeak cakes with poached eggs

SERVES 2

400g floury potatoes, such as Maris Pipers, peeled and cut into chunks (or leftover mash or roasties)
30g butter
1 leek or onion, finely sliced
A wedge of savoy or other tasty cabbage, or about 5 or 6 leaves of cavolo nero or kale, or some Brussels sprouts, shredded
Flour, to dust
2 tbsp oil, duck fat or dripping
2 free-range eggs
A few chives or parsley sprigs, snipped
Salt and black pepper

In the early days of our deli in Padstow I used to boil and bake hams and roast beef for cold pink slices. I would reduce down the boiling liquid from the hams for stock, then I'd use the fat and juices from the beef to make bubble and squeak cakes with any leftover greens and potatoes from the night before. I didn't bother to coat them with breadcrumbs – I just floured and fried them, normally in leftover dripping, and they sold exceptionally well. Here, though, with a nod to vegetarians I have used vegetable oil and butter but, if like me, you love the taste of dripping, feel free. Incidentally, we fry the chips in our fish and chip shops in dripping because they provide that comforting taste of Sunday roasts.

If not using leftovers, boil the potatoes in salted water until tender. Drain them and leave to air dry in a colander for a few minutes, then mash well. Season with salt and pepper.

Heat the butter in a pan and sweat the leek or onion and the greens over a medium heat until tender, then mix with the potatoes – if using leftover roasties, crush them first.

Form the mixture into 2 patties and dust them with a little flour. Heat the oil or fat in a frying pan and fry the potato cakes until golden on each side.

Serve each bubble and squeak cake topped with a poached egg and garnished with black pepper and chives or parsley.

Aubergine braised with soy, ginger & pak choi

SERVES 2
3 tbsp vegetable oil
2 medium aubergines, cut into thick rounds
1 garlic clove, chopped
¼ tsp chilli flakes
1 star anise
10g root ginger, peeled and grated
1 head of pak choi, cut into quarters through the bulb end
45ml soy sauce
1 tbsp runny honey
Handful of fresh coriander, chopped

To serve
Boiled rice

This is one of my assistant Portia's recipes from her time working as a young chef in Hong Kong in the mid nineties. During the break in split shifts, Mary, the kitchen porter would make this dish of extreme deliciousness for the tired chefs. Portia didn't get a recipe as she couldn't speak any Cantonese, but this is her memory of it. You could use thinly sliced white cabbage instead of pak choi.

—

Warm the oil in a frying pan or wok over a medium heat. Add the aubergine slices and fry them gently until they're golden and softened.

Add the garlic, chilli flakes, star anise, ginger, pak choi and a splash of water, then cook for a couple of minutes. Add the soy sauce and honey, cover the pan with a lid and cook for another 6–8 minutes, until the pak choi has wilted and the sauce is bubbling. If you prefer a slightly runnier and less intense sauce, add a little more water.

Sprinkle with chopped coriander and serve over boiled rice.

Beetroot, carrot & cumin fritters

MAKES 4
300g beetroot, peeled
200g carrots, peeled
½ red onion, finely sliced
½ tsp cayenne pepper
1½ tsp ground cumin
100g gram (chickpea) flour
Oil, for frying
Salt and black pepper

To serve
Green salad
Raita or yoghurt

A filming trip I made to India in 2012 absolutely sealed my affection for gram flour, which is why there are several recipes for fritters here. I guess because gram flour has so much more flavour than conventional wheat flour it transforms simply grated vegetables into something much tastier, while acting as a binding agent for making good fritters. Cumin is the perfect spice for this recipe, but do feel free to add some chilli if you so wish.

Using a coarse grater, grate the beetroot and carrots. Mix them with the red onion and season with cayenne, cumin, salt and pepper and mix well. Stir in the gram flour and add enough water to make a batter that coats the vegetables. You'll need 50–100ml, depending on the water content of the beetroots and carrots.

Coat the base of a non-stick frying pan with oil and place over a medium heat. When the oil is hot, add large spoonfuls of the mixture to the pan and flatten them a little with the back of a spatula. Fry the fritters for 3–4 minutes, then turn them over and repeat on the second side. Drain briefly on kitchen paper.

Serve with a green salad and some raita or yoghurt.

Courgette, pea & spring onion fritters

SERVES 2
300g courgettes, coarsely grated
100g frozen peas, defrosted
3 spring onions, sliced on the diagonal
Small handful of fresh mint or parsley or a mix of both, chopped
75g feta cheese, crumbled (optional)
80g gram (chickpea) flour
Oil, for frying
Salt and black pepper

To serve
Pitta or flatbreads (see p.301 if you want to make your own)
Tzatziki (shop-bought or see p.291)

I'm not a great fan of writing vegetarian or vegan recipes, but that doesn't mean I don't love dishes without meat. This recipe, which is one from my assistant Portia, is vegetarian if you use feta cheese or vegan, without the feta. The mango chutney on the side I think compensates for the of lack of umami from the cheese in the vegan version. There's a recipe for my own mango chutney on page 293, which I think is better than any you can buy – just a suggestion.

Mix the grated courgettes with half a teaspoon of salt, place them in a sieve and leave for 10 minutes to drain. Squeeze out the excess water.

Mix the courgettes with the other ingredients, except the oil, and add a tablespoon or 2 of water if needed to bind the mixture together into a thick batter.

Coat the base of a non-stick frying pan with oil. When the oil is hot, add spoonfuls of the batter to the pan and flatten them a little with the back of a spoon. Cook for a couple of minutes until golden brown, then flip them over. Transfer to a plate lined with kitchen paper and place in a low oven while you cook the rest.

Serve with warmed pitta or flatbreads and some tzatziki.

Sweetcorn, carrot & garam masala fritters

SERVES 2
150g sweetcorn, fresh, tinned or frozen
2 medium carrots, peeled and grated
1 small red onion, very finely sliced
1 tsp garam masala
¼–½ tsp chilli flakes (depending on your heat preference)
½ tsp salt
100g gram (chickpea) flour
Handful of coriander leaves, chopped
Oil, for frying

To serve
Raita and/or mango chutney
Salad

The great joy of these fritters, and those on pages 183 and 184, is the use of chickpea flour to bind them. This flour is rich in protein which makes it an important ingredient in Indian cooking. It's also gluten-free.

Mix all the fritter ingredients, except the oil, together and add up to 100ml of water to make a thick batter that coats the vegetables.

Coat the base of a non-stick frying pan with oil and place over a medium-high heat. Add large spoonfuls of the batter – about 3 at a time depending on the size of your pan – and fry the fritters for a few minutes until golden and crisp. Flip them over and fry for another few minutes. Transfer to a plate lined with kitchen paper and place in a low oven while you cook the rest.

Serve hot with raita and/or mango chutney and a salad.

Mackerel poke bowl

SERVES 2
200g sushi rice
2 tbsp rice wine vinegar
1 tbsp sugar
½ tsp salt
2 very fresh mackerel fillets, skinned and pin-boned
½ small cucumber, chopped
1 avocado, peeled, stoned and diced
50g mangetout, trimmed
2 or 3 spring onions, sliced on the diagonal

Marinade
1–2 tsp pickled sushi ginger, finely chopped
1 tbsp sesame oil
1 tbsp soy sauce
Good pinch of chilli flakes
1–2 tsp rice wine vinegar
1 garlic clove, grated

There are two very important details about mackerel for me: first it needs to be absolutely fresh, and second, the less you cook it the better. Fortunately, it's very easy to tell the freshness of mackerel because of its extraordinarily colourful blue, green and turquoise skin which is so attractive when the fish is very fresh. It is perfection in this Hawaiian poke recipe, but you could use traditional tuna if you prefer. If you want to make the pretty curls of spring onions as in the photo opposite, see the tip on page 35.

Start by preparing the sushi rice. Rinse the rice well, soak it in cold water for 30 minutes, then drain and rinse. Put the rice in a pan with 250ml of water. Cover and bring to the boil, then simmer for 10 minutes. Turn off the heat and leave the rice, covered, for another 10 minutes. Tip it into a bowl and stir in the vinegar, sugar and salt. Leave to cool completely.

Mix the marinade ingredients together in a bowl. Cut the mackerel into small pieces. Add them to the marinade, stir well to coat the mackerel and leave in the fridge while the rice cools.

Divide the cooled rice between 2 bowls and top with the mackerel and juices. Add the cucumber, avocado and mangetout in neat sections, then scatter over the sliced spring onions.

Quick as a sandwich stir-fry

SERVES 2
3 tbsp vegetable oil
3 spring onions, sliced on the diagonal
1 red chilli, chopped, or ¼ tsp of chilli flakes
1 garlic clove, sliced
250g cooked rice (about 100g dry weight)
75g prawns (or leftover cooked chicken, tofu, salmon, sausage, egg, etc)
100g spinach, peas, shredded cabbage, peppers, mangetout or mushrooms, sliced
1–2 tbsp soy sauce or black bean sauce
A small handful of coriander, chopped
Soy sauce and/or sriracha, to serve

This dish is all about using up leftovers: you need some rice, protein and an element of greenery. Spend a minute chopping and a few minutes stir-frying and you have a delicious, satisfying meal in less time than it would take to make a sandwich. The key to this, though, is that you must eat it from a bowl and with chopsticks.

Heat the oil in a wok or large frying pan. Add the spring onions, chilli and garlic and stir for about 30 seconds.

Add the rice, prawns (or other protein) and any vegetables. Stir-fry over a high heat until everything is heated through, then season with soy or black bean sauce. Scatter over the coriander and serve immediately, with some soy sauce or sriracha on the side.

Chicken saltimbocca

SERVES 2
2 skinless chicken breasts
4 sage leaves
4 slices of prosciutto
20g butter
1 tbsp olive oil
80ml dry white wine
Salt and black pepper

My mother was a great home cook and one of her favourites, and mine, was saltimbocca. The only bit of the recipe I have changed is to use chicken breast rather than veal, simply because veal is a bit frowned upon these days. My dad's choice of wine to go with this dish was Alsace Gewürztraminer.

Flatten the chicken breasts by placing each one in between 2 sheets of baking parchment and bashing them with a rolling pin until they are only about 6–8mm thick. Season with plenty of black pepper and place a sage leaf on top of each piece.

Lay out 2 slices of prosciutto side by side, place a chicken breast on top and fold the ham over. Top with a further sage leaf and secure with a cocktail stick. Repeat with the remaining chicken breast, prosciutto and sage.

In a large frying pan, melt all but a knob of the butter with the olive oil. When it's foaming, add the chicken breasts. Cook for 3–4 minutes on each side, until the chicken is cooked through and the prosciutto is crisp.

Add the white wine to the pan and bring to the boil, then add the knob of butter and allow it to bubble and thicken a little. Season with salt and pepper.

Nice with sautéed potatoes (see page 296) and perhaps some wilted spinach or fried courgettes (see page 200).

Duck breasts with spiced plum sauce

SERVES 2
200g sushi rice
2 duck breasts (about 150g each)
Oil, for brushing
Salt and black pepper

Spiced plum sauce
200g dark red plums, stoned and quartered
3 large garlic cloves, sliced
25g root ginger, peeled and sliced
2 tbsp brown soft sugar
2 tbsp red wine vinegar
2 tbsp black bean sauce
1 tbsp soy sauce

To serve
Steamed tenderstem broccoli, sugar snap peas or mangetout

Point one: I think that duck, as a rather fatty meat, goes really well with tart fruit, particularly plums. Point two: like virtually everyone else, I'm inordinately fond of Peking duck pancakes and the plum sauce which is such an essential part of the dish, so I've made a sauce to echo that. It's really important to get dark red-fleshed plums for this, otherwise the dish can look a little brown.

For the sauce, put the plums in a pan with a splash of water and cook for about 7–8 minutes over a low heat, until the plums are very tender. Add the remaining ingredients and blend until smooth.

Rinse the rice well, soak it in cold water for 30 minutes, then drain and rinse. Put the rice in a pan with 250ml of water. Cover and bring to the boil, then simmer for 10 minutes. Turn off the heat and leave the rice, covered, for another 10 minutes.

Season the duck breasts with salt and pepper. Brush a frying pan with some oil. Lay the duck breasts skin-side down in a cold pan and turn on the heat. Cook them over a medium-high heat for about 6 minutes until the skin has browned and some fat has been rendered, then turn the breasts over and cook them for a further 3–4 minutes for rare pink meat. For medium, cook for another minute to minute and a half. Set the duck aside to rest for 5–10 minutes.

Slice the duck breasts on the diagonal, spoon over the plum sauce and serve with the rice and steamed vegetables.

Salt of the earth

A long time ago in a movie I've forgotten the name of, a character offers a cigarette to a companion, who says, 'No thanks, I've given them up'. The smoker replies, 'So you plan to live for ever?' Don't get me wrong – we all plan to live for ever, or in the words of the band Marillion:

> 'Well, I gave up computer games, I gave up meat,
> I gave up watching TV in my favourite seat,
> I gave up wearing fur and I gave up wearing leather,
> But I can't give up believing that I'm going to live for ever.'

What about salt then? Surely it's quite a way down the danger scale, and in the same song Marillion mentions dangers like cocaine, smack, alcohol and crack. I guess it's just a fact of the safe little world we want to live in that nearly everyone is worried about salt now, but as my mother would have said, 'Oh, for heaven's sake'. For me, the reality is in the gospel of St Matthew:

> 'Ye are the salt of the earth: but if the salt hath lost
> his savour, wherewith shall it be salted?'

Some may contend that in the end the taste buds can accommodate giving up all but a trace of salt and apparently everything will eventually taste lovely without it. For me, however, seasoning is the most important part of my repertoire of instincts and skills as a cook. Cooking without salt is like asking a painter to paint without using the colour white. You can do it, but why? I know the chefs who work for me think that I'm really heavy handed with salt because I'm always suggesting that there's not enough in dishes, but occasionally things can be too salty.

I do think that salt is too important to leave out for dietary reasons; it's a flavour enhancer after all. A book that inspired me on this subject is Samin Nosrat's *Salt, Fat, Acid, Heat: Mastering the Elements of Good Cooking*, which is well worth reading. In fact, the worst culprits for excessive salt use are food manufacturers because they know that the mixture of salt and sugar is the ultimate and cheapest way of making

'Cooking without salt is like asking a painter to paint without using the colour white. You can do it but why?'

food taste lovely. People do say that there's more salt in a famous chain restaurant's apple pie than in their chips!

When I was in Palermo while making my *Long Weekends* series we filmed a delightful cooking sequence in the roof garden of a slightly dilapidated house. The dish we made was anelletti, the Sicilian version of lasagne, using little ring-shaped anelletti pasta rather than sheets. The cook, Viviana Randazzo, was from central casting – a passionate and demonstrative Italian mama. I questioned her about the excess of everything she was putting in the sauce – garlic, tomato, olive oil and salt – and she simply said *esagerare, esagerare*! A good cook must '*esagerare*': exaggerate.

In Greece last year at a fish restaurant called Stegna Kozas at Stegna Beach near Archangelos on the island of Rhodes, the owner Dimitris Kozas came up just as my fish soup was being served and he smothered it with olive oil and sea salt. He, too, might well have been saying 'exaggerate' because that's what salt lets you do. Coarse sea salt, particularly, induces a burst of flavour that I liken to the final movement of Beethoven's Ninth with all the cannons or indeed, looking back to my disco days, the final part of Led Zeppelin's 'Stairway to Heaven' which was when I used to switch on the strobe lights; two of them actually.

Salt is my strobe. I believe strobes are banned now.

Breadcrumbed pork with Tonkatsu sauce

SERVES 2
300g pork tenderloin cut in half diagonally
25g plain flour
1 egg, beaten
50g Panko breadcrumbs
60g clarified butter or ghee or oil
Salt and black pepper

Tonkatsu sauce
2 tbsp tomato ketchup
1 tbsp Worcester sauce
2 tsp soy sauce
½ tsp Dijon mustard
Pinch of sugar

To serve
Finely shredded cabbage
Lemon wedges

This is one of the dishes I fondly remember from what sadly has been my only trip to Tokyo. We ate lots of it in the Ginza district of the city, sitting on beer crates and drinking Asahi beer. It is, of course, a very common dish but at that time, twelve years ago, Japanese fast food was a bit of a revelation to me. I love the way that all the cafés I seem to remember were under a railway line and made to look shambolic, but actually it was all Japanese style. The sauce is really easy to make, but you can also buy it online.

Put the pieces of pork tenderloin between 2 sheets of greaseproof paper and bash them with a rolling pin until they are only about 3mm thick. Season with salt and pepper.

Mix the sauce ingredients together in a bowl and set aside.

Dip each piece of pork in flour, then beaten egg, then lastly in the breadcrumbs.

Heat the clarified butter, ghee or oil in a large frying pan and when it's hot and foaming, lower in the pork. Fry for about 3 minutes on each side until golden and crisp.

Slice the pork and serve with the finely shredded cabbage and drizzle with Tonkatsu sauce. Add some lemon wedges on the side.

Chipotle-glazed pork steaks with sweet potato mash & pineapple & tomato salsa

SERVES 2
3 heaped tsp chipotle paste or chipotles en adobo (see p.294)
1½ tsp clear honey
2 boneless pork loin steaks (about 120g each)
500g sweet potatoes, peeled and cut into cubes
Salt and black pepper

Pineapple and tomato salsa
¼ small pineapple, peeled, cored and diced (about 150g prepared weight)
1 tomato, diced
½ small red onion, finely chopped
½ red or green chilli, seeds in or out as you like, flesh finely chopped
Small handful of fresh coriander, chopped
Juice of ½ lime
Pinch of salt

Is there anyone who doesn't love the smoky taste of chipotles? In Mexico they often come with some form of pork dish and here they are in a marinade for pork chops. Incidentally, don't consider barbecuing this dish, as the glaze will just burn. I've suggested using chipotle paste, which you can get in any supermarket now, or chipotles en adobo which are chipotles in spicy tomato and onion sauce. Once you've tried chipotles en adobo you'll be hooked and I suspect they'll be available in supermarkets before too long.

Mix the salsa ingredients together in a bowl and season with a pinch of salt.

Mix the chipotle paste or chipotles en adobo and honey together in a small bowl and season with salt and pepper. Brush the pork on both sides with the mixture and set aside until ready to grill.

Boil the sweet potatoes in salted water for about 10 minutes or until tender, then drain well. Mash the potatoes and season generously with salt and pepper, then set aside to keep warm while you grill the pork.

Set the grill to a medium-high heat, baste the steaks with more of the chipotle and honey sauce and grill for 4–5 minutes, depending on the thickness. Turn the steaks over, brush with more sauce, then put them back under the grill until golden. If you have a meat thermometer, the internal temperature should be 63°C. Put the steaks on a plate and cover them with foil, then leave to rest for a few minutes.

Serve the grilled pork on the sweet potato mash and top with the pineapple and tomato salsa.

Pork loin steaks with cider & sage

SERVES 2
2 pork loin steaks (each about 180g)
Olive oil, for frying
6 sage leaves
½ onion
30g butter
50ml cider
Salt and black pepper

Fried courgettes
30g butter
1 medium or 2 small courgettes, trimmed and cut into rounds
Small bunch of chives, chopped
Salt and black pepper

To serve
Boiled new potatoes

Like lamb and mint, pork has to have sage. I have to confess that when filming in places like Spain or Italy and enjoying the delights of suckling pig, I still crave the spicy fragrance of sage and the tartness of apples, which is provided here by the cider. This fried courgette side dish is particularly good and goes well with the saltimbocca on page 190 or with grilled fish or chicken.

Season the steaks with salt and pepper. Add a splash of oil to a frying pan and fry the chops over a medium heat for about 3 minutes on each side. Transfer them to a plate and keep them warm.

Finely chop the sage and onion together or mince them in a mini food processor. Add the butter to the frying pan and gently fry the sage and onion. Add the cider, then put the pork back in the pan and simmer to reduce the sauce to a sticky glaze.

Meanwhile, melt the butter in a separate frying pan. Add the courgettes, season with salt and pepper and fry gently, turning occasionally. When they're nearly done, add the chives and continue to cook until tender.

Serve the steaks with the reduced sauce, the courgettes and some boiled new potatoes.

Schnitzel Holstein

SERVES 2

- 2 boneless, skinless chicken breasts
- 2 tbsp plain flour
- 1 egg, beaten
- 60g fine white breadcrumbs
- 4 tbsp vegetable oil
- 2 eggs
- 20g butter
- 2 tsp nonpareil capers, drained
- Juice of ½ lemon
- 4 anchovy fillets, from a tin
- Lemon wedges, to serve
- Salt and black pepper

I make this with flattened chicken breasts rather than veal, as veal is a bit out of favour and considerably more expensive. I love the accompaniments: fried eggs, lemon, anchovies and capers.

Flatten the chicken breasts by placing them between 2 sheets of baking parchment and bashing them with a rolling pin until they are only about 6–8mm thick. Season with salt and pepper. Dip each chicken breast first in flour, then in beaten egg and lastly in the breadcrumbs.

Heat half the oil in a large heavy frying pan. Carefully add the chicken breasts and cook them for about 3 minutes on each side until crisp and golden. Transfer them to a plate and keep them warm.

Wipe the pan, add the rest of the oil and fry the eggs. Top each chicken breast with a fried egg.

Wipe the pan again, add the butter and when it's foaming, add the capers and lemon juice. Swirl it all around in the pan, then spoon everything over the chicken. Top each serving with 2 anchovy fillets arranged like an X and serve with lemon wedges on the side.

Harissa lamb steaks with chickpea mash & tomato salad

SERVES 2
1 tbsp harissa paste
2 tsp olive oil
2 lamb leg steaks
Salt and black pepper

Chickpea mash
2 tbsp olive oil
1 large garlic clove, finely chopped or crushed
1 tsp ground cumin
400g tin or jar of chickpeas, drained and rinsed
Juice of ½ lemon
Small handful of coriander, chopped

Tomato salad
2 tomatoes, finely sliced
1 small red onion, finely sliced
Pinch of salt
Olive oil
Lemon juice

As I have mentioned elsewhere, I'm a late convert to mashing pulses and using them instead of potatoes, but they possess the same quality of being able to enhance whatever flavours you put with them. Here, I mash some chickpeas with garlic, lemon, cumin and coriander and also brush the lamb steak with harissa before grilling it with the aim of creating a dish with a North African flavour.

Mix together the harissa and olive oil. Season the lamb steaks with salt and pepper and brush one side of each with half of the harissa mixture.

Preheat the grill and cook the steaks for 3–4 minutes. Turn them over, brush the second side with the remaining harissa mixture and cook for another 3–4 minutes.

Heat the oil in a pan, add the garlic and cumin and cook for a minute. Add the chickpeas with 3–4 tablespoons of water and heat them through well. Mash with a potato masher or stick blender until you have the desired texture, then season with lemon juice, coriander, salt and pepper. If the mixture becomes too thick, add a tablespoon or so of boiling water.

For the salad, mix the sliced tomatoes and onion together, then add salt, pepper, olive oil and lemon juice, to taste.

Serve the lamb on top of the chickpea mash with the salad on the side.

Beef bibimbap

SERVES 2
200g sushi rice
Oil, for frying
2 carrots, peeled and cut into matchsticks
1 tsp sesame seeds
125g baby spinach, washed
100g shiitake mushrooms, sliced if large
125g sirloin or ribeye steak, seasoned and finely sliced
2 eggs
100g kimchi
Salt and black pepper

Gochujang sauce
4 tbsp gochujang
1 tbsp sugar
1 garlic clove, grated or finely chopped
1 tbsp toasted sesame oil
2 tbsp mirin or rice vinegar

This dish isn't difficult to make and it's quick to cook, but you do need to get organised and have everything to hand before you start cooking. I first tasted bibimbap in New Malden, southwest London, which could be described as Little Korea as there's that many Korean restaurants there. What makes eating in these places really special is that half the customers are Korean too.

Rinse the rice well, soak it in cold water for 30 minutes, then drain and rinse. Put the rice in a pan with 250ml of water. Cover and bring to the boil, then simmer for 10 minutes. Turn off the heat and leave the rice, covered, for another 10 minutes.

Mix together the ingredients for the gochujang sauce in a bowl and set aside.

Have a plate and some foil to hand. Add a splash of oil to a large non-stick frying pan or wok and stir-fry the carrots. Sprinkle them with some of the sesame seeds and season with salt, then remove them from the pan. Put them on a plate and cover with foil to keep warm.

Wilt the spinach in the pan with a little salt and stir in a couple of teaspoons of the sauce and the remaining sesame seeds. Set the spinach aside alongside the carrots but keep them separate. Fry the mushrooms until tender and set aside to keep warm.

Add a little more oil and get the pan really hot, then cook the sliced steak for a minute or so. Keep it warm with the vegetables while you quickly fry the eggs.

Divide the rice between 2 bowls, then divide the steak and the vegetables, including the kimchi, between the bowls in segments like spokes on a wheel. Top each serving with a fried egg and drizzle over some gochujang sauce. Serve any leftover sauce on the side.

SUPPERS WITH FRIENDS

Supper with friends immediately sounds more informal and much more fun than 'dinner party'. Nevertheless, there is slightly more preparation and cooking required for most of the dishes in this chapter than in some of the others, but not much, I hasten to add. The steak and kidney pudding (page 239), for example, does need to cook for a while, but the meat and onions don't have to be browned. You just put everything into a bowl lined with suet pastry, put it in a steamer and leave it alone. Another example is the chicken pilaf (page 230), for which the chicken needs to be marinated – hardly a very challenging task.

I know I've said this many times before, but the object of a successful supper with friends is for the cook to be able to sit down with his or her chums and not be rushing around at the last minute in a panic. There are a few gifted individuals who can finish off quite a complicated supper while talking to everyone and still staying perfectly at ease. Sadly, I'm not one of those but it is a magnificent skill. I am thinking of my friend Rowley Leigh who is quite happy talking about anything, while drinking a glass of white Burgundy and finishing off a rather complicated Italian dish of artichoke hearts cooked in olive oil, all at the same time.

I have tried. I remember cooking a paella while surrounded by lots of friends, including Stanley Tucci and his wife Felicity, and Hugh and Lulu Bonneville. My lasting memory of the occasion is that I let the rice burn, but I bet no one else noticed. For me, it's important to be ready to chat amiably to friends. I've had too many evenings when the person I most want to talk to is preoccupied with the food and not able to relax and enjoy the occasion.

If you're more like me than Rowley, make up your mind whether or not you want to cook something you can finish before your friends arrive and plan accordingly.

The evening will be better that way. This means choosing dishes that can be mostly prepared in advance, such as the puff pastry topped fish pie (page 219) or the chicken, lemon and garlic tray bake (page 224).

Some of the dishes in this chapter, though, do require a little last-minute attention from you. For instance, the steamed whole sea bass with garlic, ginger and spring onions (page 212) is really simple to cook but does need filleting before serving. And if you cook the spatchcocked chicken on page 232 you might want to bring it to the table and carve in front of your friends for a bit of theatre. But if your filleting or carving skills aren't up to much, you might prefer to keep your guests distracted and happy while you dissect the dinner in private and plate it up in the kitchen. That's what I do with Christmas dinner nowadays and no one seems to mind.

Tartiflette

SERVES 4–6

- 1kg waxy potatoes, such as Charlotte or Anya, peeled and left whole or halved if large
- 2 tbsp olive oil
- 1 large onion, sliced
- 200g smoked bacon lardons
- 2 garlic cloves, chopped or grated
- 100ml dry white wine
- 200ml double cream
- 200g Taleggio, Port Salut, Emmental or Gruyère, cut into thin slices
- Salt and black pepper

Delicious, rich and warming comfort food, this is traditionally made with Reblochon, but my version uses Taleggio, Port Salut, Emmental or Gruyère, all of which are readily available from supermarkets.

Boil the potatoes in salted water, drain them in a colander and leave until they're cool enough to handle. Cut them into thin slices.

Preheat the oven to 200°C/Fan 180°C. Heat the oil in a frying pan and gently fry the onion until soft and golden. Add the bacon lardons and garlic and fry for another few minutes. Turn up the heat, add the white wine and bring it to the boil. Then turn down the heat, add the cream and stir to combine. Season with plenty of black pepper.

Add the sliced potatoes and carefully fold them into the creamy sauce. Turn everything into an ovenproof dish, measuring about 20 x 30cm or with a capacity of 2.5–3 litres, and top with slices of cheese.

Put the dish in the oven and bake for about 15–20 minutes or so, until golden and bubbling. Serve with a salad or some green vegetables.

Steamed whole sea bass with garlic, ginger & spring onions

SERVES 6

1 x 1.5kg sea bass, scaled, cleaned and trimmed
15g root ginger, cut into fine matchsticks
4–5 spring onions, trimmed and thinly sliced
1 red chilli, finely sliced
2 tbsp dark soy sauce
2 tbsp sesame oil
4 garlic cloves, finely sliced
Handful of fresh coriander, chopped

This is my absolute favourite way of cooking a whole fish. I always think for anyone with doubts about fish, this is the dish to change their mind. It's a simple combination of freshly steamed fish, soy, ginger, garlic, sesame oil and spring onions and it makes you realise how much the Chinese love their fish. I know it's not particularly Chinese, but I like to add some sliced red chilli too. I cooked this for an episode of my Cornish series with a beautiful two-kilogram fish and demonstrated how to fillet a whole cooked fish for guests. The joke was we never actually managed to go out bass fishing, as the weather was so bad. On the programme, we played: 'Some days there just ain't no fish' by Hoagy Carmichael, which includes the following lines:

'Wish for a catch ev'ry day and you're wasting a wish,
For some days there just ain't no fish.'

Put the fish into a steamer or fish kettle or on a rack in a roasting tin and sprinkle over the ginger. Add water to a depth of about 2cm. If you are using a fish kettle, raise the rack up a little with a couple of balls of foil to lift the fish above the water. Cover with a lid or foil and steam for about 20 minutes until cooked through.

Lift the fish on to a warmed serving dish, scatter over the spring onions and chilli and cover with foil to keep it warm.

Spoon about 5 tablespoons of the cooking juices into a small pan, add the soy sauce and bring to the boil. Pour this over the fish. Heat the sesame oil in a small pan. Add the garlic, fry for a few seconds, then pour over the fish. Sprinkle with coriander and serve with tenderstem broccoli or pak choi.

Does anyone have dinner parties any more?

Could it be that very formal entertaining is a thing of the past, replaced by much more amiable and relaxed gatherings with friends? You might remember Mike Leigh's play *Abigail's Party* starring the incomparable Alison Steadman as Beverly? She organises a horribly uncomfortable event to welcome, and show off to, her new neighbours. It's laced with enjoyable sneers about what I call 'nouveaus' and my wife in her Australian way would call 'cashed-up Bogans'. During this evening I seem to remember them all listening to Demis Roussos, and Beverley offering olives around, as opposed to leaving them for people to help themselves. The people in the play remind me of minor characters in Charles Dickens's *Our Mutual Friend*, Mr and Mrs Veneering: 'They were brand-new people in a brand-new house in a brand-new quarter of London, everything about the Veneerings was spick and span and new. All their furniture was new, all their friends were new, all their servants were new ...'.

Abigail's Party was written in the 1970s. More recently we've had the TV series, *Come Dine with Me*, a programme about people hosting three-course, often terrible, dinners at home. Everyone secretly loves to watch it because the food is usually awful and it's much more about one-upmanship than enjoying a meal with friends.

But eating in company inevitably imposes a set of rules, otherwise chaos would rein. There have to be some standards to a bodily function that, I hesitate to say, is as basic as sex. There's a marvellous book by the Canadian writer Margaret Visser called *The Rituals of Dinner,* which points out that an occasion of gathering together for eating has to have rules, and as such, it's an endless source of amazement and mirth to observe the rules of others.

For instance, there's the etiquette of something like the arrangement of knives and forks to indicate that the diner has finished eating. Visser writes: 'If your fork is laid tines down in Denmark, it means you want more food: tines up expresses the end; but in Italy, forks are finally laid parallel to knives with tines *down*.' The use of chopsticks by the Chinese and Japanese, she points out, is not because they are better or worse at picking up food to deliver to the mouth, it's because they are far less dangerous than knives, which should remain in the kitchen.

For the same reason, our table knives are blunt and rounded and it's not considered acceptable to point a knife at anyone at a meal – presumably, sharp knives at the table have often resulted in bloodshed. Armed with information like this, it soon becomes clear that whether at dinner parties or simple suppers there are countless rituals about food and eating. Think of the absurd disagreement in *Gulliver's Travels* between the Big-Endians and the Little-Endians in Lilliput about which end you should break a boiled egg!

Three-course dinners at home, however, are not what I like to do, and supper is the antithesis of the dinner party. Supper is what you have with your kids, what you invite a few friends round for, or what you have on bonfire night. It's about sitting around a kitchen table with someone making pizzas in the Aga. More than anything, though, it's the joy of entertaining people in your own home. There's nothing to beat it. I love going out to restaurants, of course. Restaurants are my life, and I wouldn't still be so deeply involved with them if I didn't enjoy the euphoria of seeing so many people forgetting their troubles and revelling in the escape that is a good meal surrounded by other people all having fun too, Nothing, however, beats a meal at a friend's home. People love being invited to other people's houses and it's not about critically checking out how they live. It's the same simple feeling of the abandonment of cares and worries as going to a restaurant, but more so because it's someone's house and they have honoured you by asking you into it.

What's more, the absence of formality that supper suggests is also an invitation to relax, do what you want, get up and dance, maybe on the table. You can talk to the cook earlier on, but if it's me, I might prefer it if you didn't, even though if little things go wrong, it really doesn't matter. No one's going to care. Maybe you can play with the dogs, drink too much and demand an ancient bottle of red in the cupboard is opened. I say this because one evening recently a friend spotted a very old bottle of Château Latour in my house and urged me to open it. I prevaricated, saying it needed to breathe and should be poured into a decanter, etc, etc. He just said, 'If you don't open it now it's going to sit there for years and years. We all know Sas only drinks champagne and you'll never open it to drink on your own.' So I did. I decanted it into a jug and actually it was very nice.

That's why it's hard to sit down to a formal three-course dinner party any more, unless it's been done as a nostalgic memory. Nowadays, it's much more about your generosity in showing your friends what you're really like at home give or take a glass or two.

The last time we had some friends over for a meal it was to celebrate my stepdaughter Olivia's twenty-fourth birthday. She asked me if I would cook a paella, and would I mind making it with chorizo? I agreed of course but asked if it really did have to be with chorizo because Jamie Oliver got into a lot of bother with the Spanish who said they would never include it in a paella. Then I thought what I prat I was being and found a recipe from my Spanish series that I'd never used and included chorizo, green beans, prawns and artichoke hearts. It's not in this book as it's not simple enough and took me all day to make. I suggested some vitello tonnato for starters and she asked me what that was. 'Tuna, anchovies and veal,' I said. She asked if she could think about it. I knew she meant no thanks, so we settled on a tarte flambé – similar to the faux pizza on page 19 – that I baked as everyone arrived and cut into little squares to hand round. For pudding, I decided on the last-minute cheat's tiramisu on page 275 and served it in glasses that we use about once every three years and are kept in a box on top of the kitchen cabinets.

I think what made the night special was that it was filthy weather outside, bitingly cold with a few flurries of snow. It was so cold that I put all the beer and white wine outside on the terrace to keep chilled. There was no room in the fridge because it was stuffed with champagne, so I had to slide my baking tray of tarte flambé ready to go into the oven on top of the bottles. I pointed this out to Sas to which she replied, 'Am I bothered?' She had laid the table for fourteen people which meant we had to get two chairs out of the attic. She decorated our boardroom-sized table made of old parquet flooring with a line of little vases of spring flowers all in pastel shades and she brought out our Laguiole cutlery. It's not all in one colour, as I would have preferred when she bought them, but it has see-through handles of red, green, blue and yellow. She then put out pink place mats and pink table napkins and the lights were all turned up.

The first to arrive was Gennaro Cirillo, the assistant manager from our restaurant just across the Thames in Barnes. Gennaro has been serving drinks and making salads at our parties for some years now – so much so that he's part of the fun. He's from Puglia so everyone wants to talk to him about their holidays

As everyone else arrived, I think the contrast between the cold dark night and all the colour and warmth in the room and the smell of cheese and smoked bacon made them feel that they were going to have a good time, and indeed they did. Olive invited two friends, Emma and Kayjah who had been at Westminster Catering College with her, and everyone else was asked because they had known her for ages, like our ex next-door neighbours, David and Janette.

After the customary spat between me and Sas because I had forgotten to sort out the Sonos and it always goes wrong on party nights, it all went very well, and everyone talked to everyone else. Two more of Olive's friends from work arrived later and dancing happened very enthusiastically. The music got louder and louder and masses of expressions of affection occurred. The tiramisu was a great success and touchingly when I got up the next morning the fairies had cleaned everything up – and even put the pudding glasses back on top of the kitchen cabinets.

'Supper is what you have with your kids, what you invite a few friends round for, or what you have on bonfire night. It's about sitting around a kitchen table ...'

Puff pastry topped fish pie

SERVES 6

600ml whole milk
500g whiting, coley or pollock
300g undyed smoked haddock
2 egg yolks
2 tbsp cornflour
85g mature Cheddar cheese, grated
Splash of white wine
Large handful of parsley, chopped
150g peeled prawns, fresh or frozen and defrosted
320g ready-rolled puff pastry
Milk or egg yolk, to glaze
Salt and black pepper

I love a fish pie but I do realise that there are a lot of processes involved, although the great thing is that when you come to serving there's nothing to do except take it out of the oven. I've made this recipe as simple as possible by not having a proper béchamel sauce or mashed potato, as you would for a traditional fish pie. I made a traditional one for my family, including grandchildren, last Easter assuming everyone loved a fish pie, but that generation were not at all keen. They didn't like the mashed potato on top of the sauce. Next Easter I'll be serving fish pie like this, with a puff pastry top.

Preheat the oven to 200°C/Fan 180°C. Heat the milk in a wide pan, add the fish and poach it for 3–5 minutes. Take the pan off the heat, then lift the fish out with a slotted spoon, leaving the milk in the pan. When the fish is cool enough to handle, peel off any skin and gently break the flesh into large chunks. Allow the milk to cool a little.

In a small bowl, mix together the egg yolks and cornflour to form a paste. Gradually whisk in about a ladleful of the poaching milk. Place the pan of milk over a low heat and whisk in the egg yolk mixture, then stir over a medium heat until you have a thickened creamy sauce. Stir in the grated cheese, wine and parsley, then taste and season with salt and pepper.

Add the fish, sauce and prawns to an ovenproof dish, about 20 x 30cm in size, and gently combine. Top with the pastry and brush with milk or egg yolk. Slash the pastry a couple of times to allow steam to escape and bake for 25–30 minutes until the pastry is golden and risen. Serve with peas, broccoli or green leafy vegetables.

Crayfish & tarragon tart

SERVES 4

150g cooked crayfish tails
1 x 20–22cm savoury pastry case
2 eggs, beaten
150ml double cream
3 tarragon sprigs, leaves stripped from stalks and chopped
40g Comté cheese, grated
Salt and black pepper

To serve
Green salad

TIP

If you prefer to make your own pastry, there's a recipe on page 302. And if you are using a 23cm tart tin you will need to increase the filling a little. I suggest using 3 eggs and 250ml of cream – the rest should be fine.

This was inspired by a dish I ate at Henk de Villiers Ferreira's lovely informal restaurant at the Trevisker Garden Centre just outside Padstow. He makes individual tarts using lobster, which I feel is slightly out of the scope of simplicity, so I've used freshwater crayfish instead.

Preheat the oven to 160°C/Fan 140°C.

Drain the crayfish tails and arrange them in the pastry case.

Mix the eggs, cream, tarragon and cheese together in a bowl and season with salt and pepper. Pour the mixture into the pastry case, making sure the crayfish tails are evenly distributed. Bake in the oven for about 25 minutes or until the filling is softly set and creamy.

Leave the tart cool to room temperature and then serve with a green salad.

Salade tiède of smoked bacon, croutons & rocket with tomatoes, cucumber & avocado

SERVES 6

600g new potatoes
160g salad leaves, including rocket and frisée
½ cucumber, halved lengthways and cut into chunks
300g cherry tomatoes, halved
1 large ripe avocado, sliced
3 boiled eggs, peeled and halved (optional)
3 tbsp sunflower oil
1 garlic clove, peeled and bashed
150g lardons, Polish sausage or chorizo
250g bread, cut into croutons
1 tbsp red wine vinegar
Salt and black pepper

One of the best dishes I came across from the French bistro cooking of the seventies was the salade tiède. I used to think that it was like a Waldorf or Caesar salad – that it always had to contain smoked lardons, which I was unfamiliar with, as well as red wine vinegar, croutons, garlic and frisée. Now I realise it's just a warm salad made with whatever you've got. The only constant is that you need to fry some sort of salt pork, such as bacon, Polish sausage or chorizo, with some bread in oil, then add vinegar and let it bubble down a bit.

Cook the potatoes and cut them in half if small or quarters if larger. Allow them to cool slightly.

Put the salad leaves in a large serving bowl and scatter over the cucumber, tomatoes, warm potatoes, avocado and eggs, if using.

Add the oil to a frying pan and fry the garlic for one minute, then remove. Add the lardons or sausage and the croutons and fry until they are golden and crisp.

Add the vinegar to the pan and let it bubble to reduce for 30 seconds. Scatter the contents of the pan over the other salad ingredients and gently turn over. Serve immediately.

Chicken, lemon & garlic tray bake

SERVE 6–8

- 4 tbsp olive oil
- 12 chicken thighs, skin on and bone in
- Juice of 1–2 lemons
- 5 garlic cloves, chopped
- Small bunch of thyme, leaves stripped from stalks
- 3 courgettes, cut into thick slices on the diagonal
- 2 fennel bulbs, trimmed and sliced
- 8 new potatoes, scrubbed and cut into thick slices
- Sea salt and black pepper

I suppose I should have asked for this recipe from Lulu Bonneville, having enjoyed it at a lovely long lunch with her and Hugh (aka Lord Grantham). But what I love doing is taking someone's recipe that I really like and not copying it but just paying homage with my own version. I love getting recipes from those understated but really good cooks who manage to produce something delicious and are also so organised that they are around for the glass of champagne on arrival. They just seem to magic the food up.

Preheat the oven to 220°C/Fan 200°C.

Add a small amount of the oil to a large frying pan and place it over a medium-high heat. Working in batches, fry the chicken thighs for a few minutes until the skin has taken on a deep golden colour.

Mix the lemon juice, garlic, thyme and the rest of the olive oil in a bowl. Arrange the slices of courgette, fennel and potato in a large roasting tin and pour over two-thirds of the lemon and oil mixture. Toss to coat the vegetables and season with salt and pepper.

Arrange the chicken on top, skin-side up, and pour over the remaining lemon and oil mixture. Season the chicken with salt and pepper. Bake for 35–40 minutes until the chicken skin is crisp and golden and the vegetables underneath are tender. Nice with a green salad or green beans.

Chicken enchiladas

SERVES 4
1 small precooked chicken (about 900g), meat shredded and chopped, or leftover roast chicken
10–12 corn tortillas
Vegetable oil
60g Lancashire cheese or feta, crumbled, or grated Cheddar cheese

Sauce
400g tin of tomatoes
3 tbsp chipotles en adobo (shop-bought or see p.294)
1 medium onion, chopped
2 garlic cloves, halved
1 tsp dried oregano
2 tbsp vegetable or corn oil
Salt and black pepper

To serve
60ml soured cream
Handful of fresh coriander, chopped

In the sixties there was a song by Pat Boone called 'Speedy Gonzalez' in which Speedy is begged to stop drinking with a floozy called Flo and come home because there are no enchiladas in the ice box. When I first went to Mexico in 1968, I just had to have enchiladas and they were chicken enchiladas. This is my memory of them.

For the sauce, put the tomatoes, chipotles en adobo, onion, garlic, oregano and oil in a food processor and blend until smooth. Pour the sauce into a pan, season with salt and pepper, then simmer for 10 minutes to thicken slightly.

Pour a third of the sauce into a jug and set it aside. Add the shredded chicken to the remaining sauce in the pan and mix to coat and heat through.

Fry a tortilla in a little oil in a frying pan, then remove it and add some of the chicken filling. Roll up the tortilla and place it seam-side down in a baking dish. Repeat and once all the tortillas are packed into the dish, pour the remaining sauce down the middle of the dish and sprinkle the cheese on top. Preheat your grill to medium.

Place the dish under the grill for 5 minutes until the cheese is softened and the sauce is bubbling. Top with soured cream, scatter with fresh coriander and serve immediately.

Gratin of chicken, leek, cider & potatoes

SERVES 4
50g butter, melted
400g boneless, skinless chicken thighs, diced
2 leeks, trimmed and sliced
150ml cider
1 heaped tsp Dijon mustard
1 tsp soy sauce
¼ tsp pimentón (sweet or hot), plus extra for sprinkling
300ml double cream
350g Maris Piper potatoes, scrubbed and very finely sliced
50g Cheddar cheese, grated
Salt

To serve
Green leafy vegetables

I wrote this recipe for a series I filmed in Cornwall last autumn to tie in with a visit to a cider maker in Lerryn, near Lostwithiel. I wanted to make an all-in-one dish, as I know how popular they are, and the combination of the chicken and leeks, bound together with double cream and cider, then topped with potatoes and cheese, makes a perfect autumnal lunch or supper. It never ceases to amaze me how great good cider is in a savoury dish like this.

Preheat the oven to 180°C/Fan 160°C. You will need an ovenproof dish measuring about 26 x 20cm.

Heat half the butter in a frying pan and fry the chicken until golden. Transfer it to a plate.

Add the leeks to the pan with the remaining butter and soften them over a low heat without allowing them to colour. Add the cider, then the mustard, soy sauce, pimentón, cream and half a teaspoon of salt. Bring to the boil for 2 or 3 minutes to thicken the sauce.

Put the chicken back in the pan with any juices, then tip everything into the oven dish.

Arrange the potato slices over the filling and sprinkle over the grated Cheddar and some more pimentón.

Bake for 30–40 minutes until bubbling and golden. About 5 minutes before the end of the cooking time, preheat the grill. Put the dish under the grill to brown the top, then serve with green leafy vegetables.
Recipe photographs overleaf.

Pilaf with buttermilk chicken & pomegranate

SERVES 4
2 large boneless chicken breasts, skin on
100g buttermilk
1 garlic clove, grated
Large pinch of saffron
2–3 tbsp hot water
2 tbsp olive oil
1 onion, sliced
300g basmati rice
450ml chicken stock
1 tbsp za'atar
Handful of parsley, chopped
2 tbsp pine nuts
Seeds of 1 pomegranate
Salt and black pepper

Normally I'm not really in favour of marinating meat, unless the process involves a light cure from salt or a mild pickle from some acidity like wine or in this recipe, buttermilk. In this version of a Turkish/Persian pilaf, the buttermilk has the effect of making the chicken more tender and moist.

About 2 to 4 hours before cooking, put the chicken breasts in a bowl with the buttermilk and garlic and leave them in the fridge to marinate.

About 30 minutes before cooking, put the saffron in a bowl, pour over the hot water and leave it to bloom.

Heat the oil in a saucepan with a lid and fry the onion until soft. Add the rice and stir it into the oil. Add the saffron water and stock, then season with half a teaspoon of salt and some black pepper. Put a lid on the pan, turn down the heat and simmer the rice for 10–12 minutes until the liquid has been absorbed.

Preheat the oven to 220°C/Fan 200°C. Remove the chicken from the marinade, put it in a baking dish and sprinkle with salt and the za'atar. Cook in the preheated oven for 20–25 minutes, depending on the thickness of the breasts.

Stir the parsley and pine nuts into the rice. Slice the chicken and place it on top of the rice with the pomegranate seeds.

Spatchcocked chicken with garlic, oregano & lemon potatoes

SERVES 4

1 chicken (about 1.4kg), spatchcocked (backbone removed and flattened)
Juice of 1 large lemon
3 tbsp olive oil
2 tsp dried oregano or 1 tbsp fresh oregano leaves, chopped
½ tsp garlic salt
¼ tsp cayenne pepper
1 tsp soy sauce

Lemon potatoes

1kg potatoes, such as Maris Pipers, peeled
Juice of 1 large lemon
1 tsp dried oregano
6 tbsp olive oil
Salt and black pepper

I cooked this for my whole family in a garden attached to a traditional Lindean sea captain's house on the island of Rhodes last Easter to celebrate my seventy-fifth birthday. I wanted to make something simple and stress free, so decided on spatchcocked chicken with a marinade and some potatoes cooked with lemon and oregano in the oven. The chicken was a great success, but the potatoes less so because I used waxy salad ones. I realised while talking to some locals later that floury potatoes are much better and this recipe includes changes not only to the type of potato but also to the way they're cooked.

Preheat the oven to 200°C/Fan 180°C. Cut the potatoes into wedges the size of fat chips and put them in a medium roasting tin measuring about 20 x 30cm or with a capacity of 2.5–3 litres. Add the lemon juice, oregano and oil, season with salt and pepper, then toss the potatoes to coat them in the oil and seasonings. Pour 225ml of water into the corner of the dish (so as not to wash all the seasoning off the potatoes) and bake in the oven for about 45 minutes.

Prepare the chicken by turning it on its breast and cutting down either side of the backbone. Use strong scissors to cut through any bones. Remove the backbone and use it for stock. Turn the chicken over and press it down to flatten it.

Baste the potatoes with the juices in the tin, then put the chicken on a wire rack over the potatoes. Mix the lemon juice, oil, oregano, garlic salt, cayenne and soy sauce together, then pour this over the chicken. Put the tin back in the oven and cook for 45 minutes. Check that the chicken is done – the temperature at the thickest part should read 75°C on a probe.

Transfer the chicken to a carving plate and cover with foil to keep it warm. If the potatoes are still a bit wet, turn the oven up to 220°C/Fan 200°C and cook them for a another 10 minutes. Nice with a simply dressed green salad.

Chicken b'stilla

SERVES 6

3 tbsp olive oil
1 large onion, finely sliced
½ tsp turmeric
1½ tsp ground ginger
700g boneless and skinless chicken thighs, cut into bite-sized chunks
Large pinch of saffron strands
1 tsp ground cinnamon, plus extra for dusting
1 level tbsp icing sugar, plus extra for dusting
6 eggs, beaten
5 large sheets of filo pastry
60g melted butter
40g flaked almonds
Salt

I first wrote a recipe for b'stilla in my book Mediterranean Escapes *in 2006 and made it with pigeon. Compared to the method in my original recipe, this is indeed a simple supper, though only bordering on it. I really like this dish, mostly because it epitomises the mixture of sweet, savoury and spicy so typical of North African cooking and indeed quite a lot of Sicilian cooking too. I've heard Palermo referred to as the largest North African city outside of Africa. B'stilla also happens to be a fantastic chicken pie.*

Heat the olive oil in a large frying pan, add the onion and cook until softened. Add the turmeric, ginger and chicken and stir to coat the chicken in the spices and onion. Fry for a few minutes, then add 150ml of water and half a teaspoon of salt. Cover the pan with a lid and cook for 20 minutes.

Using a slotted spoon, lift out the chicken and set it aside. Stir the saffron, cinnamon and icing sugar into the liquid in the pan, then cook until reduced and syrupy. Season with salt. Add the beaten eggs and cook gently until you have soft, moist scrambled eggs. Set aside.

Preheat the oven to 210°C/Fan 190°C. Lay 3 sheets of filo in a 24cm diameter springform cake tin, brushing each sheet with melted butter and placing them in alternating directions. The filo will hang over the sides of the tin.

Put half the egg mixture in the tin, top with the chicken and then the remaining egg. Scatter with flaked almonds and fold over the overhanging filo and brush with butter. Top with 2 more buttered sheets of filo and tuck them in at the sides, then generously brush the top with butter.

Bake the b'stilla for 25–30 minutes until crisp and golden and sprinkle with the remaining icing sugar mixed with a little ground cinnamon.

Lamb tagine with apricots

SERVES 4
2 tbsp olive oil
750g lamb neck fillet, cut into chunks
1 onion, chopped
3 garlic cloves, chopped
2 level tbsp ras-el-hanout
400g tin of chopped tomatoes
1 tbsp honey
15 dried apricots, halved
Salt and black pepper

Couscous
400ml just-boiled water or stock
200g couscous
Handful of fresh coriander, chopped, plus extra to garnish
40g flaked almonds

This brings back memories of a trip to the North African part of Marseilles while filming my series Secret France. In order to emphasise the large number of spice shops there, I bought a large bag of ras-el-hanout which means 'head of the shop' in Arabic – sort of the top spice blend of the shop. It was a heady mixture of ginger, cinnamon, nutmeg and cloves, more akin to the spicing of medieval England and not at all like Indian flavourings. At the time I was so happy with my bag of spice, but we carried on filming and I had nothing to put it with and in the end it found itself in the back of my cupboard and it lost its sweet fragrance. A good ras-el-hanout is the centrepiece of this dish and I would recommend you buy the best you can find. The other loveliness here is the apricots and the almonds. I have chosen neck fillet simply because it is not too fatty and it's fairly quick to cook, just forty-five minutes.

Heat half the oil in a shallow flameproof casserole dish or a tagine. Working in batches so you don't overcrowd the pan, fry the lamb until browned all over, then set it aside.

Add the onion, garlic and ras-el-hanout to the pan and fry gently until softened, then add the tomatoes, honey, apricots and 200ml of water. Put the lamb back in the pan, stir and season to taste with salt and pepper. Bring to boil, cover the pan with a lid and simmer very gently for 40 minutes until the lamb is tender. If the sauce looks a little too runny, cook for a further 5 minutes, uncovered.

While the lamb is cooking, add the water or stock to the couscous and leave it to stand for 5–10 minutes. Fluff up the couscous with a fork, then stir through the coriander and flaked almonds and season with salt and pepper.

Serve the tagine on top of the couscous and sprinkle with a little extra coriander.

Toad in the hole

SERVES 4
4 tbsp oil
8 pork sausages
Salt and black pepper

Batter
130g self-raising flour
3 eggs, beaten
300ml milk

Onion gravy
40g butter
350g onions, sliced
2 tsp brown sugar
or redcurrant jelly
1½ tbsp plain flour
500ml good beef stock

Long ago when I was cooking every day in The Seafood Restaurant kitchen, toad in the hole was one of the favourite staff teas, particularly when served with an onion gravy made with beef stock. At the time, Dave Miney's toad in the hole was legendary – he's now the co-founder of Bincho Yakitori in London. I've often thought that we overlook how great our everyday British dishes, like this one, can be, particularly if the sausages are of exceptional quality. They don't have to be all-meat European ones – they can have some cereal content – but they must have a good texture and be nicely flavoured and seasoned with plenty of black pepper.

First make the batter. Put the flour, eggs and milk into a blender and season with salt and pepper. Whizz until you have a smooth batter, then leave it to rest in the fridge.

For the gravy, melt the butter in a pan and add the onions and the sugar or jelly. Cook the onions over a gentle heat for 20–30 minutes until they're soft and golden.

Meanwhile, preheat the oven to 220°C/Fan 200°C. Put the oil and sausages in a roasting tin that measures about 30 x 25cm and cook for 15 minutes until the sausages are browned. Pour the rested batter over the hot sausages in the tin and put the tin back in the oven for 20–25 minutes until the batter is risen and golden.

While the toad in the hole is in the oven, increase the heat under the onions and brown them for 5–10 minutes. When they've taken on a deep brown colour, add the flour and make a roux-like mixture. Cook this for a minute, then add the stock and keep stirring until the mixture comes to the boil and thickens. Season with salt and pepper.

Serve the toad in the hole with the gravy.

Steak & kidney pudding

SERVES 6
700g chuck steak
225g ox kidney
2–3 tbsp plain flour
1 tsp salt
1 tsp cracked black pepper
1 medium onion, chopped
Handful of parsley, chopped
Leaves from 2 thyme sprigs
2 bay leaves
Butter, for greasing
1 tbsp dark soy sauce
Beef stock

Suet pastry
350g self-raising flour, plus extra for dusting
175g shredded suet
Large pinch of salt

To serve
Steamed cabbage and boiled potatoes

A brief glance at this recipe might suggest it's not that simple, but in fact it's just a matter of putting everything in the pudding basin with a suet surround and steaming it for four hours. It's the perfect partner for great red wine.

Cut the steak into small pieces. Cut the kidney in half, snip out the white core with scissors, then cut the kidney into small pieces. Put the steak and kidney into a bowl with the flour and seasoning and toss well. Mix in the chopped onion, parsley, thyme and bay leaves.

For the pastry, mix the flour, suet and salt with 225ml of cold water to form a soft dough. Turn the dough out on to a lightly floured surface and knead briefly until smooth. Roll the dough out, using a little more flour, into a 36cm circle. Cut out a quarter of the circle and set it aside for the lid.

Lightly butter a 1.75-litre pudding basin and line it with the large piece of dough. Overlap the cut edges slightly, brushing them lightly with water and pressing them together well to seal. Spoon the meat mixture into the basin and add the soy sauce and enough beef stock to come three-quarters of the way up the meat.

Roll the reserved piece of pastry into a circle that's about 1cm larger than the top of the basin. Brush the edge with water, press it firmly on to the top of the pudding and crimp the edges together well to make a good seal. Cover the basin with a pleated sheet of parchment or a pleated sheet of foil and tie securely in place with string.

Put some sort of trivet into the base of a large saucepan, cover with about 5cm of water and bring to the boil. Put the pudding into the pan, cover with a well-fitting lid and leave it to steam for 4 hours, topping up the water now and then from the kettle when necessary. Uncover the pudding and serve it straight from the basin with some steamed cabbage and boiled potatoes. *Recipe photographs overleaf.*

SOMETHING SWEET

If you are a fan of the *Great British Bake Off* this chapter may not be for you because I have tried every which way to reduce the amount of baking you have to do to make these recipes. Wherever possible, I've used bought biscuits, pastry, ice cream, meringues and sponges. It is really all about last-minute dishes.

I have to say that this goes a little against the grain with me because, in spite of my history of cooking fish, I actually like making puddings, even more than eating them. But this book is about simple recipes – which I think also implies quick – and curiously, these puddings, with a little bit of help from shop-bought elements, sometimes turn out better than those you make from scratch.

I am thinking in particular about the cheat's tiramisu on page 275. I really love the full-blown recipe I did in my last book, *At Home*, which calls for the custard to be cooked in a bain marie so that it holds it shape. For this new version, though, I've used whipping cream and mascarpone, flavoured with Baileys, instead of custard. I've lined the base of the serving dish with shop-bought sponge and topped the whole thing with cocoa or crumbled Cadbury's flake. It takes me about 10 minutes to make and while it's not quite as luxurious, it's much lighter and fresher than the original in a fraction of the time. A similar recipe, and one that I made from scratch in my third Cornwall series, is the clementine trifle on page 282. This time I bought the sponge and custard and it takes less than half the time of the original version to make.

The other point about this chapter is that I am a great fan of light puddings with lots of fruit, so I had to have a summer berry jelly (page 251). Most of the recipes use a bit of fresh or frozen fruit and some store cupboard basics, and one of the simplest that I often fall back on is Mark Hix's Swedish iced berries with hot white chocolate sauce (page 278). I also love bananas with toffee sauce and ice cream (page 260), or just defrosted black cherries in black forest Eton mess (page 267).

Some of these puddings are my equivalent of my habitual dessert – just a scoop of ice cream from the freezer, a must-have after grilled lamb chops. A good example is the lemon posset (page 257). It has just three ingredients, cream, sugar and lemon juice and is now one of my favourite puddings. I am always keen to get it on the restaurant menus with a shortbread biscuit. Although it's full of cream, it isn't heavy and I think it's the perfect end to a meal.

A recipe from my series *From Venice to Istanbul* that I haven't published before is the Greek peach pie (page 272) made of layers of filo and fruit. It brings back memories of an orchard just outside Thessaloniki where there were a couple of trestle tables covered with red checked cloths and peaches – a celebration of peaches. There were boxes of them piled high on either side and the trees behind were laden with red and yellow fruit. On the table were glasses of peach juice and there in the centre was a baked pie filled with crackling baked filo, peaches and honey.

Lemon posset

SERVES 4
2 unwaxed lemons
125g sugar
425ml double cream

To serve
Viennese biscuits
(shop-bought
or see p.302)

This simple but delightful lemon dessert comes from a restaurant called Scaccomatto in Bologna. I have to confess I didn't try it myself there but the film crew raved about it, so I asked Mario, the chef, for the recipe. Having made it, I can see why everyone loved it. It's one of those very handy puddings you can make in advance.

Pare the zest of one of the lemons with a potato peeler and add it to a pan with the juice of both lemons (you need about 100ml) and the sugar.

Place over a gentle heat and stir to dissolve the sugar, then bring to the boil and turn off the heat

In a separate pan, scald the cream – bring it to just below boiling point – then remove the pan from the heat. Pour the cream on to the lemon syrup and mix well.

Pour the mixture through a sieve into a clean bowl or jug, then divide between 4 glasses or coffee cups. Allow to cool, then refrigerate for at least 4 hours before serving with crisp biscuits. *Recipe photographs overleaf.*

Bananas with toffee sauce & ice cream

SERVES 4
3 or 4 bananas, peeled
85g butter
40g brown soft sugar
2 tbsp double cream
2 tbsp dark rum

To serve
Vanilla ice cream

Sas, my wife, has to have bananas in the house because if you are endlessly on a diet they are what you eat most of the day. Trouble is that she doesn't eat them nearly as often as she says she does and they go black in the bowl in the kitchen. As someone who hates waste, I sometimes slice the bananas and dry them out in a low oven – they are actually really good like this, as it concentrates the sweetness. Other times, when it's clear that the bananas are not going to be eaten, I use them to turn a bowl of ice cream into something truly spectacular. Who wants more banana bread? Not me!

Cut the bananas on the diagonal into thick slices.

Melt 20g of the butter in a frying pan and fry the bananas until golden but not mushy, then tip them on to a plate.

Add the remaining butter to the pan with the sugar, cream and rum, then stir until everything comes together in a sauce.

Add the bananas to the sauce and gently turn them until they are coated all over. Spoon the bananas and sauce over servings of ice cream and enjoy immediately.

My pantry

In my last book *At Home*, I had a lot of fun writing a piece about what I actually found in my store cupboard. I thought it would be amusing and would strike a chord with lots of other people, particularly with reference to out-of-date ingredients which should have been thrown away long ago. But here I want to make more of a recommendation on what you will need, mostly in the form of dry goods, to make the recipes in this book. You will, of course, need to buy fresh meat, fish and vegetables.

I'm aware that if you only cook one of the dishes in the book once you might think it's a bit of a waste to buy the ingredients listed here – more of that later – but for me, the overall idea of simple cooking comes with a parallel requirement to add some basic ingredients to your cupboards. Paradoxically, some of the simplest dishes can be hard to execute well. It's like an artist drawing a circle, you need a lot of training to do it. However, you can make your life very much easier, if the ingredients you need for a simple dish are on hand.

Here are my suggestions for store cupboard staples, plus a list of extras you might find useful for particular recipes in this book:

'You can make your life very much easier, if the ingredients you need for a simple dish are on hand.'

FRIDGE
Bacon, chorizo, ham.
Butter, crème fraiche (because it keeps for so long), milk, yoghurt.
Cheddar, Gruyère, Parmesan.
Duck or goose fat.
Eggs.
Pouches of chicken and beef stock.

FREEZER
Broad beans, peas, spinach, sweetcorn.
Filo pastry, puff pastry sheets, tortilla wraps.
Pouches of chicken and beef stock.
Summer berries, vanilla ice cream.

SPICES & DRIED HERBS
Black pepper, cardamom, cayenne, chilli flakes, cinnamon, cloves, coriander, cumin, curry leaves, curry powder, dried oregano, fennel seeds, garam masala, nutmeg, pimentón, saffron, salt, star anise, turmeric.

SAUCES
Horseradish, mayonnaise, mustard (English and French), nam pla (Thai fish sauce), soy sauce, tomato ketchup, Worcestershire sauce.

TINS, JARS & POUCHES
Anchovies, artichoke hearts, beans (borlotti, butter beans, haricot), black olives, capers, chickpeas, chopped tomatoes, coconut milk, custard, roasted red peppers, sweety drop peppers, tomato purée, tuna, vac-packed lentils.

CUPBOARD
Chocolate: dark chocolate, white chocolate.
Flour: cornflour, plain flour, self-raising flour.
Nuts: almonds, ground almonds, walnuts.
Oil: olive oil, sunflower oil, vegetable oil.
Panko breadcrumbs.
Pasta and noodles: egg noodles, rice noodles, short pasta (penne, orzo), spaghetti.
Rice: arborio, basmati, jasmine, long-grain, sushi rice.
Stock: stock cubes, vegetable bouillon powder.
Sugar, jam, etc: golden syrup, honey, lemon curd, peanut butter, sugar (brown and white).
Tea and coffee.
Vanilla extract and vanilla pods.
Vinegar: balsamic, cider vinegar, red wine vinegar, white wine vinegar.
Wine, cider, sherry.

EXTRAS FOR SPECIFIC RECIPES
Cheeses: Dolcelatte, feta, goat cheese, halloumi, Lancashire, mascarpone.
Spices, sauces and pastes: black bean sauce, black mustard seeds, chipotles en adobo, chipotle paste, harissa paste, ras-el-hanout, sriracha sauce, za'atar.
Miscellaneous: chana dal, condensed milk dried porcini, duck confit, ginger nut biscuits, macadamia nuts, meringue nests, savoury pastry case, sponge fingers, vegetable suet.

Once you have got these ingredients and you have made the dish, don't just let them sit there, think of other things you can do with them. Get creative in other words. Here are a few ideas for some of the ingredients on the previous page.

Artichoke hearts, roasted red peppers and sweety drop peppers: add to pasta sauce or pizza or use as nibbles with an olive oil and vinegar dressing.
Black bean sauce: add to any Chinese stir-fry or fried rice; it's so delicious, I could eat it out of the jar with a spoon.
Breadcrumbs: use to make a lovely treacle tart. Make a filling with roughly 4 times the weight of golden syrup to breadcrumbs. Add some lemon juice and zest and put the mixture in a shop-bought pastry case. Bake at 180°C/Fan 160°C for about 25 minutes.
Chana dal: a great thickener for soups.
Chipotles en adobe: add to any Mexican dish or use to spice up mayonnaise.
Chorizo: add to your fried eggs for breakfast or throw some into a Bolognese sauce.
Coconut milk: great in a soup or added to rice pudding.
Condensed milk: if you can stop eating it out of the tin with a spoon, it's delicious with fruit or in rice pudding.
Dried porcini: good addition to any stew but particularly useful in vegetarian stews as they add a smoky depth of flavour.
Filo: use to make a lovely pie with wilted spinach, crumbled feta, salt, pepper, mint or dill; brush with olive oil and bake until crisped to perfection.
Garam masala: add to anything you want to have an Indian flavour, even scrambled eggs.
Halloumi: fry it and serve with honey and walnuts.
Mascarpone: use it like cream with a pud or stir into a pasta sauce.
Orzo pasta: another great thickener for soups.
Puff pastry: makes great cheese straws. Roll it out thinly, sprinkle with grated Parmesan and add a second layer. Cut into strips and twist along the length, then bake. A sprinkle of cayenne pepper is nice too.
Ras-el-hanout: this turns any stew into a tagine; add some fruit as well, such as prunes.
Sponge fingers: do I need to say this? Eat with a cup of tea; ditto ginger nuts!
Star anise: great in mulled wine.
Vegetable suet: make dumplings for a stew and add any herbs, mustard or cheese.
Za'atar: great as a dry marinade; also, good sprinkled on roasted veg.

Finally, as I have mentioned, I don't like use-by dates and throwing things away. With some ingredients, the older they are the more boring they'll taste but you might find a lot of years may pass before you finally have to throw them out. My trick is to write a date way after the recommended use-by date on the jar or tin in felt-tip pen. This is when I ought to really be throwing it out, but I never do until I have bought a replacement.

Mint choc chip no-churn ice cream

SERVES 4–6
200g After Eights or other thin mint chocolates (fridge cold)
600ml double cream
250g sweetened condensed milk

The name is quite a tongue twister but this is so easy to make. There's so much condensed milk in the mixture that you don't need to churn it because there won't be any ice crystals. This is the sort of ice cream that Sas, my wife, might suggest us having after a stir-fry. I'll instantly agree and then when she gives me a bowlful of it I'll say it's far too much – but it isn't!

Finely chop the chocolates – this is much easier to do when they're really cold.

Lightly whip the cream and whisk in the condensed milk to combine. Add the chopped chocolate and stir the mixture really well to distribute the little shards throughout the mix.

Pour the mixture into a freezer-proof container, cover with a lid and freeze overnight.

Remove from the freezer 10 minutes before serving to allow the ice cream to soften.

Black Forest Eton mess

SERVES 2–3
200g fresh, frozen or canned cherries
15g caster sugar, to taste
1 tbsp kirsch or vodka
200ml double or whipping cream
2 shop-bought meringue nests, broken into bite-sized pieces
1 chocolate flake, crumbled, or 40g dark chocolate, grated

When I first opened The Seafood Restaurant in Padstow, the one dish that I would never consider putting on my menu was black forest gateau. The reason being that every other restaurant in Cornwall, or so it seemed, featured it, as well as a starter of prawn cocktail and steak Diane as a main course. I was far too cool for that school. Such is the nature of things, though, I now really like black forest gateau and particularly this simple spin on it.

In a small pan, cook the cherries with the sugar (if needed), until you have a slightly thickened syrupy, jammy mixture. Allow to cool completely, then add the kirsch or vodka.

Whip the cream very lightly until it is just starting to thicken. Fold it through the cherry mixture very lightly to create streaks through the cream like raspberry ripple ice cream, then add the meringue.

Divide between glasses and top with the crumbled or grated chocolate. Serve immediately – if you leave this standing, the meringue will start to dissolve.

Blackberry & apple sponge pudding

SERVES 4
Knob of butter, plus extra for greasing
550g cooking apples, peeled, cored and chopped
150g blackberries (frozen are fine)
75g caster sugar

Sponge
60g butter, softened
100g caster sugar
Zest of 1 lemon
2 eggs, beaten
140g self-raising flour
4 tbsp milk

To serve
Custard or cream

I suppose I should have called this Eve's pudding or something posh, but actually it's the sort of thing my mum would make for lunch or dinner, as we called it in those days. She would use some blackberries that she'd picked on a walk and a few windfalls from under the apple trees in the garden, then add some butter and sugar and a simple lemony sponge. We used to have a pudding at lunch every day. Now, this would be something to finish off a simple supper.

Butter a dish (about 20 x 15cm) and preheat the oven to 190°C/Fan 170°C.

Put the apples, blackberries, sugar and the knob of butter in a pan with about 50ml of water. Cook over a medium heat for 5–10 minutes until the fruit has softened, then tip it into the buttered dish.

For the sponge, cream the butter and sugar with the lemon zest. Whisk in the eggs, then fold in the flour and add the milk. Spread the sponge mixture over the fruit and bake for 35–45 minutes until golden and springy to the touch.

Serve with thick custard or cream.

Chocolate cups

MAKES 8 ESPRESSO CUPS
175g dark chocolate, chopped
300ml double cream
1 tbsp espresso coffee
1 large egg

To serve
Biscotti

You will think an espresso cup is too small, but these are so rich and smoothly delicious it'll be quite enough.

Set a heatproof bowl over a pan of barely simmering water, making sure that the bottom of the bowl doesn't touch the water.

Put the chopped chocolate and cream in the bowl and stir together until fully melted, then stir in the coffee.

Add the egg and whisk for a minute over the heat until fully incorporated. Pour the mixture into espresso cups and refrigerate for an hour or so, before serving with biscotti.

If the chocolate cups are very cold, take them out of the fridge while you eat your main course so they can come up to room temperature.

Greek peach pie

SERVES 6

- 10 good-sized ripe peaches (skin on), stoned and cut into small pieces
- 4 tbsp runny honey
- 1 vanilla pod, split
- 7 sheets of filo pastry
- 70g butter, melted
- Icing sugar

I discovered this wonderful pie when making my Long Weekends *series a few years ago, but, amazingly, it never made it into the book. Here it is now and I'm very pleased to report that it is very simple indeed and much greater than the sum of its parts.*

Put the peaches in a pan with the honey, vanilla pod and 2 tablespoons of water. Cover the pan with a lid, place it over a medium heat and cook the peaches for about 15 minutes until they have softened and started to break down. Remove the lid and continue to cook until the liquid has reduced and has a jammy consistency. Leave to cool for 10–15 minutes.

Preheat the oven to 190°C/Fan 170°C. Brush a sheet of filo with melted butter and use it to line a 20cm cake tin, with some filo hanging over the sides of the tin. Repeat with 4 more sheets of buttered filo, alternating the direction of each sheet.

Remove the vanilla pod and pile the filling on top of the filo sheets, then level it out with the back of a spoon. Fold the pastry that's hanging over the edges of the tin over the filling and brush it with butter. Finish with the remaining sheets of filo, tucking it in around the outside of the pie. Brush the top with the remaining butter.

Bake the pie for 30–35 minutes until golden brown and crisp on top. Allow to cool to room temperature before dusting with icing sugar and cutting it into 6 wedges. Nice with a dollop of Greek yoghurt.

Last-minute cheat's tiramisu

SERVES 4

- 150ml whipping or double cream
- 250g mascarpone, at room temperature
- 40g icing sugar, sifted
- 50ml Baileys or Marsala
- 150ml espresso coffee, cooled
- 8–12 sponge fingers or 4 trifle sponges
- Cocoa powder, for dusting or a chocolate flake, crumbled

Obviously there is nothing that can beat a proper tiramisu, but this is so quick and so lovely and it really does take just minutes to make.

Lightly whip the cream in a bowl until it's only just starting to thicken.

Whisk the mascarpone with the Baileys or Marsala to soften, add the icing sugar, then fold this mixture into the cream.

Pour the coffee into a separate bowl. Dip the sponges into the coffee and then divide half of them between 4 glasses or small bowls.

Add half the cream mixture, again dividing it between the bowls, then repeat the layers of sponge and cream. Dust generously with cocoa powder or crumbled chocolate.

Refrigerate until ready to serve or serve immediately if making at the last minute.

Mango & passion fruit fool

SERVES 4
1 medium-sized ripe mango, peeled and stone removed
3 passion fruits, seeds and pulp scooped out and reserved
200ml double or whipping cream
100ml Greek yoghurt
30g icing sugar, sifted

To serve
Shortbread or ginger biscuits

I wrote this for my wife Sas, as she often feels homesick for Aussie mangoes and passion fruit, but also because I love a fool. My mother used to make them with blackcurrants or gooseberries. I think you need some tartness which is where the passion fruit comes in and these days I always include the seeds, as I really like the crunchiness of them.

Put the mango flesh in a food processor and purée until very smooth. Mix with the passion fruit seeds and pulp.

Lightly whip the cream to soft peaks and fold together with the yoghurt and icing sugar. Stir the mixture through the fruit, then spoon it into 4 glasses or teacups.

Refrigerate until ready to serve with some biscuits alongside.

Mark Hix's Swedish iced berries with hot white chocolate sauce

SERVES 4
300g white chocolate buttons
300ml double cream
500g frozen berries (raspberries, blueberries, blackcurrants and redcurrants but not strawberries)

I love Mark Hix's cooking – simplicity with intelligence is how I would describe it. This dish dates from his time as head chef at The Ivy in London. What everyone loves about it is the way the hot white chocolate sauce melts the berries just enough so that they are soft on the outside but with a little frozen crunch in the middle. If you can only get a mix of frozen berries with strawberries, remove the strawberries and use them for something else. They don't work well here.

Place a heatproof bowl over a pan of simmering water, making sure the bottom of the bowl doesn't touch the water.

Place the chocolate and cream in the bowl and leave for 10–15 minutes, stirring occasionally until fully melted and warm. Turn off the heat.

Five minutes before serving, put the berries into bowls or on plates and leave them at room temperature to defrost slightly. Pour over the warm white chocolate sauce and enjoy immediately.

White chocolate & macadamia blondies

MAKES 9 SQUARES
125g butter
175g brown soft sugar
2 medium eggs, beaten
1 tsp vanilla extract
¼ tsp salt
140g plain flour
100g macadamia nuts, roughly chopped
90g white chocolate, roughly chopped

Another one for Sas. Macadamia nuts are such a big thing in Australia and they make a great combo with white chocolate. These are really simple to make and great with a scoop of ice cream or for a tea time treat.

Line a 20cm square tin with baking parchment. Preheat the oven to 180°C/Fan 160°C.

Melt the butter in a pan, remove the pan from the heat, then add the sugar and stir well. Add the eggs, vanilla extract and salt and mix well.

Add the flour and stir to combine, then fold in the chopped nuts and chocolate. Scrape into the prepared tin and bake for 25–30 minutes until a skewer comes out clean.

Allow to cool completely before cutting into squares. Eat on their own or with ice cream.

Clementine trifle

SERVES 8

- 200g Madeira cake, sliced, or 6–8 trifle sponges (shop-bought or see p.303)
- 4–5 tbsp Grand Marnier or Cointreau
- 3–4 tbsp marmalade
- 8 clementines or 3–4 oranges
- 900ml fresh thick custard (or make custard with custard powder)
- 300ml double or whipping cream
- 2 tbsp flaked almonds, lightly toasted

This is a simplified version of a recipe I wrote for my TV series Rick Stein's Cornwall to celebrate an aquavit made from an apple spirit flavoured with, and yes this is correct, hogweed. It's produced in Cornwall by a company called Howl & Loer, which in Cornish means sun and moon. In the recipe I have suggested using Cointreau or Grand Marnier, but actually if you can get hold of this spirit, called Hogweed Seed, it is really interesting: slightly bitter, slightly woody and indeed, according to the producers, with notes of clementine. The other point about this trifle is that it's incredibly collapsible. When being filmed making it, I was filled with doubt because of its delicacy and worried that trifle lovers who like to slice their trifle would find it ridiculous. For me, though, trifle is like tiramisu, the fluffier the better.

Lay the slices of cake or sponges into the base of a glass trifle bowl. Sprinkle them with 2 or 3 tablespoons of the liqueur and spread over the marmalade.

Take a thin slice off the top and bottom of each clementine or orange. Using a sharp knife follow the curves of the fruit to remove the skin and the pith. Then slice the fruit into rounds, reserving any juice. Arrange the rounds of fruit around the sides of the bowl so that they look like wheels through the bowl. Top the sponge with any juice and remaining fruit.

Stir the rest of the liqueur into the custard, then pour on to the sponge base. Lightly whip the cream and smooth it over the custard. Scatter over the toasted almonds and refrigerate until ready to serve.

Chocolate fridge cake
Mosaiko

SERVES 6

- 3 tbsp icing sugar
- 2 tbsp liqueur, such as Metaxa, Grand Marnier or even Baileys
- 225g dark chocolate, 54–70%
- 110g butter
- 5 tbsp double cream
- 170g Petit-Beurre, Rich Tea or Nice biscuits, roughly broken
- 50g walnuts, roughly chopped
- Pinch of ground allspice

TIP

If you don't want to make a roll, line a 20cm cake tin with baking parchment and press the mixture into it. Refrigerate as above, then cut into wedges to serve.

You may have noticed mosaika in refrigerated cabinets in restaurants anywhere in Greece. To me, it's a bit like sticky toffee pudding in the UK in that it's absolutely bound to please everyone. It's simply walnuts, chocolate, biscuits and a few other ingredients moulded into a cake, then refrigerated and sliced. Serve up with a bit of jam and some ice cream and it's the perfect make-ahead pudding.

Mix the icing sugar and the liqueur together in a bowl.

Put the chocolate, butter and cream in a heatproof bowl. Set the bowl over a pan of simmering water, making sure the bottom of the bowl doesn't touch the water, and stir until the chocolate has melted and the mixture is smooth. Stir in the icing sugar and liqueur, then fold in the biscuits, walnuts and allspice and mix without crushing the biscuits. Cover the bowl and leave to cool, then put it in the fridge for about an hour until the mixture has firmed up.

Line a board with baking parchment, tip the contents of the bowl on to it and shape the mixture into a rough roll. Using the parchment, roll into a neat sausage shape, measuring about 18–20cm long. Keep rolling to smooth the surface. Refrigerate overnight if possible.

Unwrap the roll. Using a butter knife dipped in hot water, smooth the outside and cut the roll into 6 thick slices. Enjoy on its own or top each serving with a ball of vanilla ice cream and drizzle with cherry jam loosened with a tablespoon or so of just-boiled water.

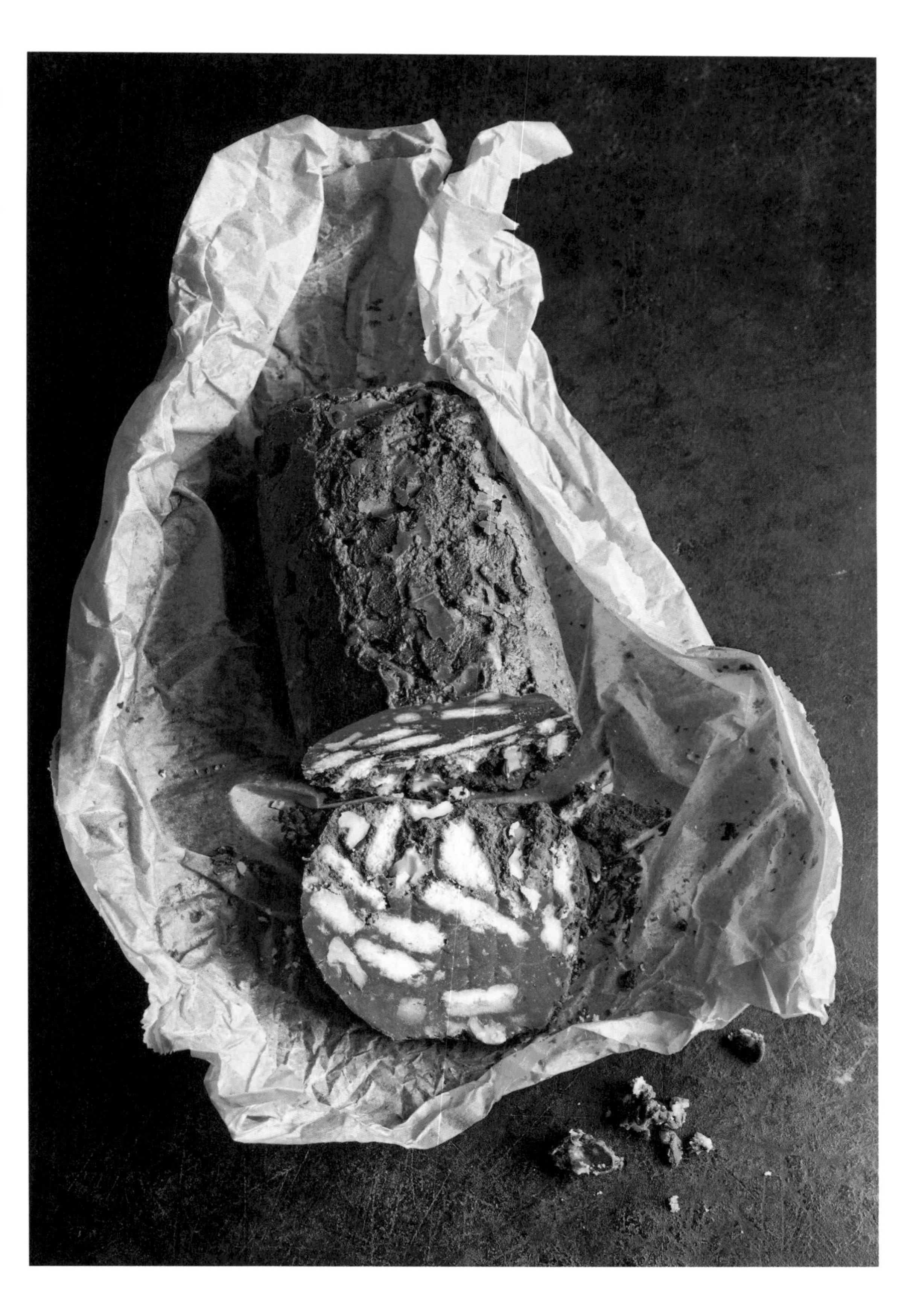

Fruited tea loaf

MAKES 1 LOAF
300ml strong tea, made with 3 Earl Grey or English Breakfast teabags
350g mixed dried fruit, such as raisins, sultanas, chopped dates, currants, mixed peel, etc.
Zest of an unwaxed lemon
Butter, for greasing
2 medium eggs, beaten
200g light brown soft sugar (or 100g caster and 100g dark brown soft sugar)
250g self-raising flour
1 tsp mixed spice

To serve
Butter
Jam

This recipe was inspired by a visit to the Tregothnan Tea Estate, overlooking the Fal Estuary and just up from the King Harry Ferry, where I filmed for my series Rick Stein's Cornwall. *The quality of tea grown there, in what I would have thought was too cold a climate, was astonishing and I used it in this tea loaf. I find it hard not to finish a meal with a little something sweet and I'm fond of a slice or two of this with butter plus, dare I suggest, jam.*

Make the tea in a pot or jug and allow it to steep for about 10 minutes. Put the dried fruit and lemon zest in a bowl and pour over the hot tea. Cover the bowl and leave the fruit to soak for a couple of hours or overnight.

Preheat the oven to 180°C/Fan 160°C. Grease and line the base of a 1 litre loaf tin (about 23 x 12 x 7cm) with baking parchment. Beat the eggs and sugar together in a bowl, then stir in the flour, mixed spice and soaked fruit and mix well.

Pour the mixture into the greased and lined tin and bake for 1¼–1½ hours until a skewer comes out clean. Leave to cool in the tin for 15 minutes, then turn the loaf out on to a wire rack to finish cooling. Serve sliced with butter and jam.

SIDES AND BASICS

Aioli

MAKES ABOUT 175ML

This is a punchy sauce, traditionally made from just olive oil, garlic and soaked dry bread, but an egg yolk is normally used these days. It is usually served with fish or stirred into fish stews but also goes well with rice dishes, grilled lamb and vegetables.

4 garlic cloves, peeled
½ tsp salt
1 medium egg yolk
125ml sunflower oil
50ml extra virgin olive oil

Mash the garlic to a paste with the salt.

Scrape the garlic paste into a bowl and add the egg yolk. Whisk everything together, then very gradually whisk in the oil, a few drops at a time at first, to make a thick mayonnaise-like mixture.

Harissa paste

MAKES A BOWLFUL

1 roasted pepper, from a jar
1 tsp tomato paste
1 tsp ground coriander
Pinch of saffron threads
½ tsp chilli flakes
¼ tsp salt

Put all the ingredients into a food processor and blend until smooth. Transfer to a bowl and cover. This keeps well in the fridge for 3 or 4 days.

Cucumber & mint raita

MAKES A BOWLFUL

175g unpeeled cucumber, halved lengthways
1 tsp salt
275g natural yoghurt
½ tsp caster sugar
2 tbsp chopped mint leaves
1 tsp fresh lime juice
Black pepper

Using a teaspoon, scoop out the seeds from the cucumber, then grate the flesh. Toss the grated cucumber with the salt, tip it into a sieve and leave to drain for 20–30 minutes.

Mix the drained cucumber with the remaining ingredients, adding a little extra salt, lime juice and pepper to taste. Eat soon after making.

Tzatziki

MAKES A BOWLFUL

The crux of a good tzatziki is to use an authentic Greek, full-fat sheep yoghurt. I don't think low-fat ones work. I also insist on eating this straight away while it's at its perfect best.

1 large cucumber
2 garlic cloves, peeled
500g Greek sheep yoghurt
75g spring onions, trimmed and finely chopped
2 tbsp chopped fresh dill or mint
2 tbsp extra virgin olive oil
1 tsp white wine vinegar
Dill or mint sprigs or cucumber slices, to garnish (optional)
Salt and black pepper

Peel the skin of the cucumber away in strips – you want to leave some but not all of it. Coarsely grate the cucumber, pile it into the centre of a clean tea towel and squeeze out most of the excess liquid.

Mash the garlic to a paste with the salt.

Tip the yoghurt into a bowl and stir in the cucumber, garlic paste, spring onions, dill or mint, olive oil, vinegar, then season with salt and pepper to taste. Serve garnished with dill or mint sprigs or a few peeled cucumber slices, if you like, then serve at once.

Quick hollandaise sauce

MAKES 250ML

225g butter
2 egg yolks
Juice of ½ lemon
Good pinch of cayenne pepper
¾ tsp salt

First, clarify the butter. Put it in a small pan and leave it over a low heat until it has melted. Then skim off any scum from the surface and pour off the clear golden liquid into a bowl. Discard the milky white solids that will have settled on the bottom of the pan.

Put the egg yolks, lemon juice and 2 tablespoons of water into a blender or food processor. Turn on the machine, then slowly pour in the warm clarified butter until the sauce is thick. Season with the cayenne and salt.

Everyday mayonnaise

MAKES 300ML

1 whole egg or 2 egg yolks
2 tsp white wine vinegar
2 tsp hot English mustard or Dijon
¾ tsp salt
300ml sunflower oil

The simplest way of making this is to put a whole egg, the vinegar, mustard and salt in a food processor. Turn on the machine and very slowly trickle the oil through the hole in the lid until you have a thick emulsion.

To make the mayonnaise by hand, make sure all the ingredients are at room temperature and use 2 egg yolks, rather than a whole egg. Put the egg yolks, vinegar, mustard and salt into a mixing bowl and rest the bowl on a damp cloth to stop it moving around. Lightly whisk to break up the yolks and, using a wire whisk, beat in the oil, a few drops at a time, until it is all incorporated.

Once you have added the same volume of oil as the original mixture of egg yolks and vinegar, you can add the oil a little more quickly. This keeps in the fridge for at least 2 weeks.

Coriander chutney

MAKES ABOUT 6 PORTIONS

Far too often this green chutney is not freshly made, and I think it only works when it is. I've taken the liberty of adding a tad more sugar than most but it doesn't half work well with the lime juice. I can't think of a curry that it doesn't go with.

Large handful of mint leaves
Large handful of coriander leaves
2 fresh green chillies, roughly chopped
1 small onion, roughly chopped
1½ tsp sugar
¼ tsp ground cumin
2 tsp lime juice
¼ tsp salt

Tip all the ingredients into a food processor and blend to form a rough paste. Serve freshly made.

Sweet mango chutney

MAKES ABOUT 10 PORTIONS

I'm still a fan of shop-bought British mango chutney. This is similarly sweet but it's slightly sharper too, and the slices of mango are a little firmer. Great with any curry.

100g sugar
100ml white wine vinegar
300g mango flesh (from firm mangoes), cut into 2cm slices
1 small onion, finely chopped
10g root ginger, finely grated
1 garlic clove, finely crushed
1 tsp whole cumin seeds
1 tsp ground Kashmiri chilli powder
½ tsp salt

Put the sugar and vinegar in a pan, place over a medium heat and stir to dissolve the sugar.

Add all the remaining ingredients and simmer over low-to-medium heat, stirring occasionally, for 45 minutes to an hour, or until reduced down to a jammy consistency.

Spoon into a sterilised jar. This keeps for about 2 weeks in the fridge.

Chipotles en adobo

MAKES 1 X 370G JAR

8 chipotle chillies
150ml just-boiled water
3 large ripe tomatoes, roughly chopped
1 medium onion, roughly chopped
4 large garlic cloves, sliced
60ml cider vinegar
¾ tsp salt
2 tsp brown sugar

Wash the chillies, remove the hard stems but leave the seeds in place. Put the chillies in a bowl with the just-boiled water and cover with cling film. Leave the chillies to soak for about 20 minutes.

Remove 3 of the soaked chillies and put them in a food processor or blender. Add the tomatoes, onion, garlic, vinegar, salt, the soaking liquid and the sugar, then process to make a smooth paste. Tip the paste into a pan and add the remaining whole soaked chillies.

Bring to the boil, then reduce the heat and simmer the chillies for about 1 hour. Check them every 20–30 minutes and add a little more boiling water if needed.

Leave to cool slightly, then pour into a sterilised glass jar. Cool completely and store in the fridge for up to a month.

Chipotle crema

SERVES 2–4

2 chipotles en adobo (see left or shop-bought), finely chopped or mashed with a pestle and mortar
2 tbsp soured cream
2 tbsp mayonnaise
Squeeze of lime juice
Pinch of salt

Mix all the ingredients together and set aside.

Tomato sauce

MAKES ABOUT 600ML

6 tbsp extra virgin olive oil
4 garlic cloves, finely chopped
1kg well-flavoured tomatoes, peeled or 2 x 400g tins of tomatoes
Salt and black pepper

Put the olive oil and garlic into a saucepan and place on the heat. As soon as the garlic starts to sizzle, add the tomatoes and simmer gently for an hour, breaking up the tomatoes as they cook. Season with salt and pepper.

If not using the sauce immediately, leave it to cool, then chill and refrigerate or freeze for later use.

Hand-cut chips

SERVES 4

500g Maris Piper potatoes
300ml olive oil
Salt

Peel the potatoes and cut them into chips by hand. They look better if they aren't too uniform.

Heat the oil in a frying pan to 170°C and shallow-fry the chips for about 10 minutes, turning them a few times. They don't need to be covered in oil. Drain, sprinkle with salt and serve.

Sautéed potatoes

SERVES 4

700g floury potatoes, such as Maris Pipers or King Edwards, peeled
50g butter
3 tbsp olive oil
Salt and black pepper

Cut the potatoes into 2cm cubes and put them in a pan of well-salted water. Bring to the boil, then simmer until tender. Drain well and leave until the steam has died down and the potatoes have dried off a little. Heat the butter and oil in a large, heavy-based frying pan. Add the potatoes and toss them repeatedly over a medium heat for 10 minutes until they are crisp, dry, sandy and light brown. The outside of the potatoes should break off a little as you sauté them to give them a nice crumbly crust.

To make sure the potatoes aren't too greasy, blot the pan with kitchen paper to remove any excess oil. Season at the last minute with salt and black pepper.

Celeriac & potato mash

SERVES 4

450g floury potatoes, such as Maris Pipers or King Edwards, peeled
450g celeriac, peeled
50g butter
50ml milk
1 garlic clove, crushed or grated
Salt and black pepper

Cut the potatoes and celeriac into chunks, put them in a saucepan and cover them with water. Bring to the boil, then turn the heat down and simmer for 15–20 minutes. Drain in a colander and return to the pan.

Mash the potatoes and celeriac with a potato masher or with an electric hand whisk, then add the butter, milk and garlic and combine. Season with salt and black pepper.

Quick dauphinoise potatoes

SERVES 6

900g floury potatoes, such as Maris Pipers or King Edwards, peeled
300ml double cream
300ml whole milk
1 garlic clove, crushed
Freshly grated nutmeg
15g butter, for greasing
Salt and black pepper

Preheat the oven to 200°C/Fan 180°C. Slice the potatoes very thinly by hand, on a mandolin or in a food processor.

Put the cream, milk and garlic into a large non-stick saucepan and season with plenty of salt and pepper. Add the sliced potatoes and simmer for about 10 minutes until they are just tender when pierced with the top of a small, sharp knife. Stir them now and then, but be very careful not to break up the slices. Season with freshly grated nutmeg and salt and pepper to taste.

Lightly butter a 1.5-litre shallow ovenproof dish. Spoon in the potatoes and liquid, overlapping the slices in the top layer neatly if you wish. Bake for about 20–25 minutes or until golden and bubbling. Allow to stand for about 5–10 minutes before serving.

Steamed fluffy rice

SERVES 4

350g basmati, jasmine or long-grain rice

Put the rice in a pan with 600ml of water. Quickly bring to the boil, stir once, then cover with a tight-fitting lid and reduce the heat to low.

Simmer basmati rice for 10 minutes and jasmine or long-grain rice for 12–15 minutes. Turn off the heat and leave to steam, covered, for a further 5 minutes. Uncover, fluff up the grains of rice with a fork, then serve.

Pilau rice

SERVES 4

2 tbsp sunflower oil
3 cloves
3 green cardamom pods, cracked
5cm piece of cinnamon stick
1 bay leaf
350g basmati rice
400ml just-boiled water
½ tsp salt

Heat the oil in a saucepan. Add the cloves, cardamon pods, cinnamon stick and bay leaf and cook gently over a low heat for 2–3 minutes until the spices start to smell aromatic.

Stir in the basmati rice and fry gently for a minute. Add the water and half a teaspoon of salt and quickly bring to the boil. Stir once, cover with a tight-fitting lid and cook over a low heat for 10 minutes.

Remove the saucepan from the heat and leave undisturbed for 5 minutes. Uncover, fluff up the grains with a fork, then serve.

Carrots à la fermière

SERVES 6

1kg large carrots, sliced into rounds
1 tsp salt
30g butter
30g flour
Small handful of flatleaf parsley and tarragon, chopped
Juice of 1 lemon
2 tsp caster sugar
Black pepper

Put the carrots in a pan of water and season with a teaspoon of salt. Cook the carrots for 12–15 minutes until tender but not soft, then drain and reserve the cooking water.

Melt the butter in a large frying pan and whisk in the flour. Gradually add about 250ml of the cooking liquid, whisking all the time to avoid lumps. Add the chopped herbs and plenty of black pepper, bring to the boil and boil for 2 minutes to thicken.

Add the lemon juice and sugar, then put the carrots back in the pan and cover loosely with a lid. Leave a small gap to allow some steam to escape. Add a little more of the cooking water, then simmer over a very low heat for 30 minutes or so. Stir gently from time, but take care not to break up the carrots. When cooked, they should be soft and coated in the glistening sauce.

Braised peas

SERVES 4

30g butter
1 onion, finely chopped
100g smoked bacon lardons
2 tsp plain flour
200ml chicken or vegetable stock
450g frozen peas
¼ tsp sugar
Salt and black pepper

Melt the butter in a pan and cook the onion and bacon for about 5 minutes over a low heat until the onion has started to soften. Stir in the flour and cook for a minute or so, then add the stock and bring to the boil.

Reduce the heat and add the peas. Cover the pan with a lid and cook for 15–20 minutes. Check the peas during the cooking time and add a little more water if necessary; the peas should be just submerged in the liquid while cooking. The finished dish should have a slightly soupy consistency.

Season with the sugar, salt and plenty of black pepper.

Steamed spinach

SERVES 4–6

900g spinach, well washed
25g butter
A few rasps of nutmeg
Salt and black pepper

Put the spinach in a saucepan, cover and place over a high heat. Stir gently as the leaves wilt down. Tip the spinach into a colander and lightly press out the excess water with the back of a wooden spoon.

Melt the butter in the pan, add the spinach and season with nutmeg, salt and black pepper. Toss briefly over a high heat and serve immediately.

Green salad

SERVES 4

2 lettuces, such as soft round, little gem, batavia or butterhead

French dressing
½ garlic clove, peeled
2 tbsp good red wine vinegar
1 tsp Dijon mustard
½ tsp sugar
8 tbsp olive oil
Salt

For the dressing, put the garlic clove on a board and lightly crush it with the side of a knife. Sprinkle the garlic with a pinch of salt, then mash it with the blade of the knife until smooth. Put the garlic into a small jug and add the vinegar, mustard and sugar. Whisk briefly, then gradually whisk in the olive oil and ¼ of a teaspoon of salt.

Split the lettuces into separate leaves and wash and dry well in a salad spinner. Put the leaves in a salad bowl and toss with 3 tablespoons of the dressing. Serve the rest of the dressing on the side – any that's left over keeps well in the fridge for a few days.

Kachumber salad

SERVES 4

4 large tomatoes, very thinly sliced
1 shallot, very thinly sliced
2 tbsp chopped coriander
¼ tsp ground cumin
Pinch of cayenne pepper
1 tbsp white wine vinegar
Salt

Layer the ingredients in a large shallow dish in the order in which they are listed, finishing with the vinegar and salt. Don't mix the salad, just leave it to stand until ready to serve.

Greek flatbreads

MAKES 8

500g strong flour, plus extra for rolling
12g salt
2 tbsp olive oil
1 sachet of fast-action dried yeast
270ml warm water

Put the flour, salt, olive oil and yeast in a bowl. Add the warm water and mix together to make a soft dough. Transfer to a lightly floured surface and knead the dough for about 4 minutes.

Put the dough back in the bowl, cover and leave somewhere warm for about an hour until doubled in size. I use my convection oven turned down to 30°C.

Divide the dough into 8 pieces and shape each one into a ball. Roll each ball on a lightly floured surface into a thin disc about 22cm across, then cover and leave for 10 minutes. Preheat the oven to 240°C/Fan 220°C. Brush the flatbreads with a little water and bake for 5 minutes. Wrap them in a tea towel to keep warm until ready to serve.

Walnut bread

MAKES 1 LOAF

600g wholemeal flour
10g fast-action dried yeast
15g salt
450ml lukewarm water
20g melted butter, plus extra to grease
1 tbsp black treacle
40g walnut pieces
2 tsp sesame seeds

Put the flour in a bowl and add the yeast, salt, water, melted butter and black treacle. Knead by hand until you have a smooth, elastic dough, then add the walnuts right at the end. You can, of course, do this in a stand mixer.

Lightly grease a 900g loaf tin. Put the dough in the tin, cover with a tea towel and leave in a warm place (about 30°C) for about 45 minutes or until the dough has doubled in size.

Preheat the oven to 230°C/Fan 210°C. Sprinkle the sesame seeds over the loaf and bake in the centre of the oven for 30 minutes. Remove from the tin and leave to cool on a wire rack.

Viennese biscuits

MAKES ABOUT 20–25

Our food stylist, Jan Smith, made these light, crumbly biscuits to go with the lemon posset on page 257.

250g really soft butter
1 tsp vanilla extract
220g plain flour
50g icing sugar
30g cornflour
Pinch of salt
Icing sugar

Preheat the oven to 200°C/Fan 180°. Line 2 large baking trays with non-stick baking parchment.

Beat the butter until really light and fluffy, then beat in the vanilla. Sieve in the flour, icing sugar, cornflour and salt and beat again until well mixed and you have a sticky dough.

Transfer the mixture to a piping bag fitted with a large star nozzle and pipe rosettes, circles or fingers on to the baking trays. Aim for biscuits about 5cm in diameter and space them well apart to allow for spreading.

Alternatively, roll the mixture into walnut-sized balls and flatten slightly once on the trays. The mixture is sticky so you will need cool hands.

Bake for 10–15 minutes, checking them after 10 minutes. The biscuits should be pale golden brown. Leave them to cool on the trays. Sprinkle with icing sugar before serving.

Rich shortcrust pastry

MAKES ENOUGH FOR 1 X 23CM TART CASE

225g plain flour, plus extra for dusting
½ tsp salt
55g chilled butter, cubed
55g chilled lard, cubed
1½–2 tbsp cold water

Sift the flour and salt into a food processor or a mixing bowl. Add the chilled butter and lard and process or work together with your fingers until the mixture looks like breadcrumbs.

Stir in the water until the mixture comes together into a ball. Turn the dough out on to a lightly floured work surface and knead briefly until smooth. Roll out and use as required.

For a slighter leaner and more malleable pastry, reduce the butter and lard to 45g each.

Trifle sponge

MAKES 1 X 23CM SPONGE CAKE

Butter, for greasing
3 eggs
85g caster sugar
85g self-raising flour

Preheat the oven to 190°C/Fan 170°C. Grease a 23cm round cake tin and line it with baking paper.

Crack the eggs into a bowl and whisk them with the sugar until very pale and creamy. Sift in the flour and carefully fold it in to retain as much air and lightness as possible.

Pour the batter into the prepared cake tin and bake for 20–25 minutes until risen and golden. Remove from the oven and leave to cool. Cut into strips to use for the trifle on page 282.

Custard

SERVES 6

400ml milk
300ml double cream
4 egg yolks
2½ heaped tbsp cornflour
2½ heaped tbsp caster sugar
2–3 tbsp Grand Marnier or Cointreau (optional)

Pour the milk and double cream into a pan and bring to the boil. Beat the egg yolks, cornflour and sugar together in a bowl, then gradually whisk in the hot milk and cream.

Rinse the pan if there are milk solids left in the bottom, then pour the mixture back into it. Cook over a low heat, stirring constantly, for about 5 minutes, until the mixture has thickened. Take care not to let the custard boil or it will curdle.

Stir in the liqueur if using the custard for the trifle on page 282. You can also use this as a pouring custard but you might want to add a little more milk or cream to get the consistency you want.

Vegetable stock

MAKES ABOUT 2 LITRES

2 large onions
2 large carrots
1 celery head
1 fennel bulb
1 garlic bulb
3 bay leaves
1 tsp salt

Wash and roughly slice the vegetables; you don't need to peel the garlic. Put the vegetables and the remaining ingredients in a large pan with 3 litres of water and bring to the boil.

Simmer for an hour, then strain the stock through a fine sieve. You may like to reduce the volume by simmering the strained stock. If not using immediately, allow to cool, then refrigerate or freeze for later use.

Fish stock

MAKES ABOUT 1 LITRE

1kg fish bones and heads (lemon sole, brill and plaice are all good but any fish is fine, except oily ones like mackerel, sardines, herrings, salmon and tuna)
1 onion, chopped
1 leek, washed and sliced
1 fennel bulb, sliced
100g celery, sliced
1 thyme sprig
30ml sunflower oil
100ml white wine

Cut up the fish bones into 5–6cm pieces and put them in a large pan. Add the vegetables, thyme and oil. Put a lid on the pan, place it over a medium heat and cook everything gently for 5 minutes, not allowing it to colour. Add the white wine and 2.25 litres of water and bring the liquid just to the boil, then turn the heat down and simmer very gently for 20 minutes.

Strain the stock through a sieve and use as required. If not using immediately, leave to cool, then chill and refrigerate or freeze. You may like to reduce the volume by simmering the strained stock.

Chicken stock

MAKES 1.5 LITRES

Bones from 1.5kg uncooked chicken or 500g chicken wings or a leftover carcass and bones from a roast chicken
1 large carrot, roughly chopped
2 celery sticks, roughly sliced
2 leeks, washed and sliced
2 fresh or dried bay leaves
2 thyme sprigs

Put all the ingredients into a large pan with 2.5 litres of water and bring to the boil. Skim off any scum that rises to the surface. Leave to simmer gently for about 2 hours – don't let it boil as an emulsion will form and make the stock cloudy.

Strain the stock through a fine, sieve and use as required. If not using immediately, leave to cool, then chill and refrigerate or freeze. Or simmer the strained stock to reduce further before storing.

Beef stock

MAKES ABOUT 2.4 LITRES

2 celery sticks, roughly chopped
2 carrots, roughly chopped
2 onions, roughly chopped
900g beef shin
2 bay leaves
2 thyme sprigs
1 tbsp salt
2 tbsp vegetable oil (if making a rich brown stock)

For a pale brown stock, put all the ingredients, except the bay leaves, thyme and salt, into a large pan with 5 litres of water and bring to the boil. Skim off any scum that rises to the surface. Simmer for 2½ hours, adding the herbs and salt for the last 15 minutes. Strain the stock through a fine sieve into a clean pan.

The stock is now ready to use, chill or freeze for later use, or you can continue to cook to reduce the liquid and make a richer stock.

For a richer-tasting brown beef stock, start by heating 2 tablespoons of vegetable oil in the pan. Add the vegetables and beef and fry for 10–15 minutes until nicely browned. Then add the water and cook as above, adding the herbs and salt 15 minutes before the end of cooking.

Recipe finder

CHICKEN & DUCK

MEAT

SIDE DISHES

COLD PUDDINGS

WARM PUDDINGS

BAKES

SAUCES

CHUTNEYS

STOCKS

Index

D

E

F

G

V

W

Y

Z

COOK'S NOTES

Generally, I don't specify the weight of garlic cloves, tomatoes, carrots or onions because the reality of cooking is that you just take a clove or two of garlic or a whole onion. However, in case it's helpful, I thought it would be sensible to suggest the weights (unpeeled) I have in mind.

1 garlic clove: 5g
1 small onion: 100g
1 medium onion: 175g
1 large onion: 225g
Small handful of fresh herbs: about 15g
Large handful of fresh herbs: about 30g

All teaspoon and tablespoon measurements are level unless otherwise stated and are based on measuring spoons:

1 teaspoon: 5ml
1 tablespoon: 15ml

Readers in Australia will need to make minor adjustments, as their tablespoon measure is 20ml.

Oven temperatures
We have given settings for regular and fan ovens throughout the book. Should you need gas settings, they are as follows:

°C	°C FAN	GAS
120	100	½
140	120	1
150	130	2
160	140	3
180	160	4
190	170	5
200	180	6
220	200	7
230	210	8
240	220	9

Eggs and chicken
Use medium free-range eggs in the recipes, unless otherwise specified. And use free-range chicken if possible.

Temperature probe
I use a temperature probe to determine the correct internal temperature of meat, poultry and fish. This is a cheap gadget and you get far more accurate results than by relying on cooking times alone. Always bring meat and poultry up to room temperature before cooking.

Bear in mind that meat and fish continue to cook after being removed from the heat; their temperature rises by about 6°C. Meat and poultry benefit from resting after being cooked and before serving.

ACKNOWLEDGEMENTS

I would like to thank everyone at Ebury for what is a great team but particularly Joel Rickett, managing director, Lizzy Gray, deputy publisher, and Albert DePetrillo, publishing director, my editor, Nell Warner, and my long-term publicist and now head of publicity, Claire Scott.

Talking of 'teams', a word which I've only recently come to accept but now quite like, thanks to Portia Spooner for her enormous contribution to the recipes, and to James Murphy for the unending great photography – we first started working together in 1999. For the fabulous way the book looks, thanks to Alex and Emma Smith. Next, I have to say with some amusement thanks to Penny Markham who yet again provided the perfect kitchen and tableware props but she was a little disappointed to have been asked to contribute so little but that is down to the extreme simplicity of the photography. I have to thank two very talented cooks, Aya Nishimura and Jan Smith, for cooking most of the recipes in the book for photography. Thanks again to James Murphy's assistant Lucia Lowther for the great lunches we all enjoy on photography days.

It was great to be working again with project editor Jinny Johnson who in addition to pointing out mistakes and inconsistencies is a good cook herself and invaluable as a second opinion as to whether a recipe should go into the book or join the 'also ran' list. Thanks to my PA Viv Taylor for keeping everyone in touch and who also enjoyed taking down dictations of many of the essays I've written for this book and suggesting bits and bobs.

Finally, the biggest thanks to my wife Sas who has been such a guiding force for this book, particularly in insisting on me looking at what young people, notably my stepchildren Zach and Olive, do actually cook for their simple suppers.

I would also like to mention all those who contributed to these recipes whether actively or by their inspiration: Lulu Bonneville; Scaccomatto Restaurant, Bologna; Olive Burns; Sara Parker Bowles; Kewpie's Restaurant, Kolkata; Kalypso Restaurant, Lindos, Rhodes; Hank de Villiers Ferreira, Trevisker's Kitchen, Padstow.

Finally, I would like to thank the following, whose wise words I have quoted in this book:

Jane Grigson, *Fish Cookery*, published in 1973 by Penguin

Margaret Visser, *The Rituals of Dinner*, published in 2017 by Penguin

John Harris, *The Natural Gardener: A Guide to the Ancient Practice of Moon Gardening*, published in 2022 by Rowman & Littlefield

4

BBC Books, an imprint of Ebury Publishing
20 Vauxhall Bridge Road, London SW1V 2SA

BBC Books is part of the Penguin Random House group of companies whose addresses can be found at global.penguinrandomhouse.com

First published by BBC Books in 2023
www.penguin.co.uk

A CIP catalogue record for this book is available from the British Library

ISBN 9781785948145

Printed and bound by L.E.G.O. S.p.A.
Vicenza, Italy

Penguin Random House is committed to a sustainable future for our business, our readers and our planet. This book is made from Forest Stewardship Council® certified paper

Deputy publisher: Lizzy Gray
Editor: Nell Warner
Home economist: Portia Spooner
Design and art direction: Smith & Gilmour
Photographer: James Murphy
Project editor: Jinny Johnson
Food stylists: Aya Nishimura & Jan Smith
Prop stylist: Penny Markham
Photography assistant: Lucia Lowther
Food styling assistant: Hanna Miller
Proofreader: Elise See Tai
Indexer: Hilary Bird